OPERATION: THRIVING MARRIAGE

A FIELD MANUAL
FOR MAXIMUM PERFORMANCE
AND PREVENTATIVE MAINTENANCE

BRYON AND JENNIFER HARVEY

WESTBOW
PRESS®
A DIVISION OF THOMAS NELSON
& ZONDERVAN

WestBow Press books may be ordered through booksellers or by contacting:

WestBow Press
A Division of Thomas Nelson & Zondervan
1663 Liberty Drive
Bloomington, IN 47403
www.westbowpress.com
844-714-3454

Interior and Exterior Author Photos Credit: Pamela McCormick Photography
Cover Design Credit: Carl Johnson of Saint Creative

ISBN: 978-1-6642-0600-7 (sc)
ISBN: 978-1-6642-0601-4 (hc)
ISBN: 978-1-6642-0599-4 (e)

Library of Congress Control Number: 2020918117

Print information available on the last page.

WestBow Press rev. date: 11/10/2020

CONTENTS

INTRODUCTION

This book is the product of years of learning about marriage. Not only are we married and have learned a lot about marriage through our personal experience, our professions have given us the opportunity to see the beauty and mess in other people's marriages.

Bryon served in church ministry for over 20 years. He wrote and taught marriage classes that helped people build healthier marriages. He counseled people individually on how to strengthen their marriages. Together we have spent countless hours counseling couples as they prepare for marriage. Bryon is also a first sergeant in the Michigan Air National Guard. As a first sergeant he has counseled many airmen on their marriages. Counseling in the military has given him a perspective that many church leaders never receive. People that come to the first sergeant may or may not share our Christian faith. They come to Bryon not because of his degree or his role in the church but rather as a fellow airmen a little further on in the journey that can mentor them.

Jen is a lawyer. Her experience as a lawyer has shown her aspects of marriage that many people only get to see in their own marriages. She has been hired by clients to represent them in divorce. She has seen marriages end. She has seen marriages restored. As an attorney that deals with trusts and estates she has also seen marriages struggle in ways that divorce attorneys never see. A friend of ours often says that the family dynamics come out most clearly and weddings and funerals. Dealing with the funeral aspect she has seen those dynamics up close and personal and how they affect marriages and families.

Together we have seen a lot of marriages and learned a lot about what works and what does not.

As we were doing research for this book we noticed that from the

Christian perspective there are a lot of books preparing couples for marriage. There are a lot of books designed to help couples in crisis. This book is neither of those. This book is for couples that have been married 3 - 10 years that are looking to strengthen their marriages. In our experience, by the time couples are in crisis it is often too late to help. The roots of the crisis occurred much earlier and if those issues had been addressed then the crisis would never have happened. We hope this book will help you address the little things in your marriage now before they become big things later. Song of Solomon 2:15 says:

Catch the foxes for us,
the little foxes,
that ruin the vineyards –
for our vineyard is in bloom (NET).

It is our prayer that this book will help you catch the little foxes in your marriage and strengthen your relationship so that you will have a thriving, healthy, and holy marriage that lasts a lifetime.

Thank you for reading; we pray that the Lord and these ideas on marriage His way strengthen your marriage,

Bryon & Jen

CHAPTER 1

WHY ARE YOU MARRIED?

In 2007, Tyler Perry produced the movie *Why Did I Get Married?* The plot revolves around four couples, all long-time friends, who take a vacation together. When the infidelity of one of the friends is revealed, it causes a cascade of revelations and conflicts regarding their marriages. These revelations leave the couples asking themselves and each other, "Why did I get married?"

Perhaps you find yourself asking that same question. "Why did I get married?" The question may have been caused by a fight you've had. It may have been caused by seeing the marriage of a friend or family member falling apart. It may just come from healthy self-reflection as you continue to follow Christ and become more like Him.

Whatever the reason, "Why did I get married?" is a pretty common question. It is very common after having been married a few years to take stock of your life and marriage and evaluate the situation. At this point the excitement of being newlyweds has transitioned to a different kind of relationship. The demands of work, running a household, and perhaps children now require a different level of attention and have shifted some of your focus. Your relationship has changed. Together you have formed patterns and habits, some healthy and others less so, that allow you to concentrate on other areas of life. Asking "Why did I get married?" is a normal and common question.

While a perfectly normal question, this question is not a particularly useful question. The question is backwards looking. It addresses something that you cannot change, whether you want to or not. Why you got married then has little relevance on your marriage now. A better question is, "Why are you married?"

So, why are you married? Yes, we know you're married because at one time you got up in front of a pastor or some other official and made a vow and then signed some legal documentation. But seriously, why are you _still_ married? Take a moment to seriously think about this question.

Most people don't think about why they are still married. At least they don't until they start thinking about not being married. They just stay married because that's what you do. Or they don't stay married because they no longer want to be married. But you're reading this book because you care about keeping your marriage healthy and strong. So, why are you married? Is it because you're madly in love with your spouse? Are you still married because of the kids? Do you like the social status of being married? Are you afraid of being alone? Is divorce just too expensive? You might even want to write your answer in the margin of this book or as a note if you're using an e-reader.

For many people reading this book: _you don't know why you're still married_. In many cases, the idea of not being married hasn't occurred to you. You're happy or at least content in your marriage. You're getting enough of what you want out of marriage and don't have a desire for that to change.

On one level, we think that's a good thing. We aren't interested in you thinking about ending your marriage. We don't want to mess up a good thing. Yet, thinking about why you're married is a good thing too. Socrates said, "The unexamined life is not worth living." It's not worth living because you miss out on much of the purpose and fulfillment of life. We think this is true for marriage as well. Moreover, we think that knowing why you are married will help keep you married and bring you a fuller, healthier marriage.

Others of you are still married because that's what you're supposed to do. You don't have any particular reason to be married but you don't have a reason not to be married either (that is, no reason to stay married but no reason to get divorced, either). Perhaps you're simply existing together or you just haven't thought about why you are still married.

But we think if you want a thriving, marriage that is going to last the rest of your lives you need to know why you're married and have a clear vision and purpose for why you should stay married. Our goal in the next few chapters is to remind you of God's purpose for marriage and give you a vision for your marriage that will help to keep your marriage strong for the rest of your lives.

In a military operation, the first step is to understand the situation and the desired end state. A commander will want information about the landscape, the people (hostile, friendly, and neutral), and the political situation. They will also need to know the desired end state. Otherwise, how will the commander and the troops know when they have been successful? The first few chapters of this book will provide that understanding for *Operation: Thriving Marriage.* In these chapters we will help you assess the current context of your marriage and help you develop a vision for where your marriage is headed. Unlike a military operation, there is no end state. The goal is for you to have a thriving marriage that will last a lifetime. We will, however, give you tools to keep pushing your marriage to be the marriage that God intends for you.

The chapters later in this book will give you tools to fulfill that vision and purpose for your marriage. In military terms, these are the tactics. We are going to discuss skills and actions that will help you respond to the context you currently find your marriage in and move towards the thriving marriage that you desire and God desires for you.

We have seen a lot of marriages that are not thriving. We have seen a lot of marriages end. When people walk into Jen's office to talk about divorce, one if not both of the spouses can only think about why they don't want to be married anymore. They have no idea why they should stay married.

As you look at why you're married, it's important to acknowledge that your relationship has changed over the years. Every relationship does. It's normal. It's unavoidable. Most of the time, it's healthy.

All living things are in a constant state of change. They are either growing or dying. The same is true of your marriage. Your marriage is either growing or dying.

We say this because as you think about why you're married, you're going to think about why you got married. That is going to make you think about what your marriage used to be like. For most of us, we have fond memories of the early days of our marriage. They honeymoon. The first home. The first home-cooked meal. All those firsts were exciting and fun. The 1500th or 2000th home-cooked meal is not as exciting as the first. The 100th or 200th week of marriage is different from the first or second.

It is tempting to look back at those times with nostalgia and want to have those feelings back. It is tempting to romanticize the those first weeks together and think that is what marriage is supposed to be. It is tempting to think that the reason to be married is to experience those feelings perpetually.

Thoughts like that are a recipe for disaster. First, it's impossible to maintain those early feelings in marriage. Relationships change whether we want them to or not. Freezing a marriage like Han Solo[1] in carbonite is not why you should be married. Second, those initial feelings were never intended to last. Those feelings, instead, set the foundation for a deeper, stronger, more fulfilling love later. Would you rather be like the couple that is happy after 50 days of marriage or the couple that is happy after 50 years of marriage. The right *why* will lead you to the right *how;* then God and your commitment to each other can finally give you the right *what*: a thriving marriage that lasts a lifetime.

In our time working with couples, reading the research, studying Scripture and our experience in our own marriage, we have found three reasons why we are still married and why we think you should be married:

1. To experience the mature, fulfilling love and joy that God intends for you.
2. To grow to be more like Jesus.
3. To represent God to the people around you and give them a glimpse of his kingdom.

---

[1] If you don't get the reference, we're very sorry for you. Your life is clearly lacking in important cultural exposure. But that's ok. We're here to help. Watch Star Wars V - The Empire Strikes Back. Then watch episode VI - Return of the Jedi so you know what happens to Han Solo. Then watch the rest of the Star Wars movies just because they're awesome. Except Episode I. For some reason, no one likes Episode I.

Mature Fulfilling Love

In his book, *The Meaning of Marriage*, Tim Keller argues, "Real love, the Bible says, instinctively desires permanence."[2] We agree with Dr. Keller's assessment. One way to look at the Bible is to see it as a love story. God is love as manifested through his complete, eternal, loving relationship in the Trinity. Throughout the Bible, God is constantly looking for His people: a community to love who will love him back. Starting from the time Adam and Eve chose their own wants over loving God in Genesis until the conclusion of Revelation when "God's home is now among his people! He will live with them, and they will be his people. God himself will be with them" (Revelation 22:3 NLT), God has been looking for permanent love.

The same is true of the humans in the Bible. Repeatedly they reach out to God for a love that is permanent. The problem, of course, is that they continually reject the unconditional, unfathomable, permanent love of God through their own sin and wickedness. Love desires permanence. Mature, fulfilling love is permanent.

Permanence, however, is not a value in itself. The promise of permanence goes much deeper than simply longevity. When you first meet someone, you never reveal all of yourself. You don't know how safe they are. Will they reject you if they know your true self? This is true no matter the relationship, whether professional, social, or romantic. You always wear a mask.

As we're writing this, we are in the middle of the global COVID-19 pandemic. Currently where we live everyone is required to wear some sort of mask when they are in any building other than their own homes. The masks do not protect us from getting the virus. The masks only protect those around us from being infected if we are unknowing carriers of the virus. The metaphorical masks we wear in relationships are intended to work in the opposite way. They do not protect the people around us from the dark parts inside of us. Rather, they are intended to protect our true selves from the wickedness in others.

These metaphorical masks may keep our true selves from being hurt

---

[2] Timothy Keller, *The Meaning of Marriage: Facing the Complexities of Commitment with the Wisdom of God*, (New York, NY: Penguin Publishing Group, 2011, Kindle Edition) 78.

by others. They also, however, prevent our true selves from being loved by others. When our true selves are locked away behind a mask, those from whom we wish to receive love never have access to us to give us the love we want and need. The masks ultimately do not protect us from being hurt but rather prevent us from being healed by the love of those who care for us.

Permanent love allows you to remove the mask. Layer by layer you take off the costume you have put on throughout your lifetime. Ultimately you get to the point where you stand before your spouse naked and unashamed (Genesis 2:25).

We dated seven years before we got married. By the time we got married, we knew each other very well. When we got married we thought we knew everything about each other. We thought we had completely removed our masks. Perhaps we had. Perhaps you had by the time you got married as well.

But here's the rub. We have changed over the past 17 years of our marriage. With every change we are tempted to put on a new costume. Sometimes we do. The permanence of our love allows us to accept each other when we put the mask back on and gives us the courage to take it back off again.

Permanent love lets you relax and be yourself. It gives you peace, comfort, and courage. Permanent love allows you to be completely known by another person and know another person completely. There is no other relationship that God has ordained that creates the context for such transparency and peace. We are still married because love desires permanence and, other than the love of God, marriage is the only relationship we have found that provides permanent love.

To Be More Like Jesus

There is a pervasive myth in our culture today that says that marriage is all about personal happiness. This can be seen in how people begin their dating and courtship relationship. It starts by finding someone to whom I am attracted. We go out on a date and I determine that this person adds something of value to my life. I decide I want to spend the rest of my life with this person because I love them and they make me happy.

Then there seems to be an unwritten clause in the marriage contract.

We have never heard it said in any marriage vows. But the clause seems to state, "I will be faithful and loyal to you as long as I am happy, fulfilled, and my needs and wants are met." If those conditions are not met spouses often get divorced. Michigan, where we live, is a no fault divorce state. In other words, anyone can legally get a divorce for any reason or no reason at all. There are hoops to jump through and it's expensive but the barriers to divorce are all financial; there are no legal barriers. Our American culture has completely bought into the myth that marriage is about happiness and state governments have made it legal. If you're not happy in your marriage, end it.

Marriage was once thought of as the foundation of society. Marriage was the place where societal and cultural values were transmitted to the next generation. Marriage was once the place where people revealed and received unconditional love and security. Marriage was about commitment to ideals higher than the individual and even ideals higher than the married couple.

These values have eroded. Marriage is, therefore, considered a relic of the past or redefined into an ideal that fits the individual. Such a philosophy is doomed to failure because there are two in the marriage rather than one, so there can never be a marriage where the individual ideals can be completely one-sided. For those in American culture who still think marriage should continue, it is not because it is the locus of love and security. It is, rather, the locus of sex and romance.

Marriage, however, does not have its endgame as personal happiness. Marriage is, rather, about personal holiness. You should not stay married to become happier. You should stay married to become holier. Indeed, society's lie of marriage equaling personal happiness is actually played out as a fleeting happiness. Abiding in Christ brings holiness and therefore lasting joy. The product of our deep connection to Jesus is love, *joy,* peace, patience, kindness, goodness, faithfulness, gentleness, and self-control (Galatians 5:22-23). We can experience this fruit of the Holy Spirit by abiding in Christ. Combine that with two like-minded spouses and their joy is robust, sustainable, and apparent to all. Pursuing holiness leads to ultimate happiness. Pursuing happiness leads to disappointment as happiness is a temporary feeling that disappears. That is why we don't say we want you to have a happy marriage. We say we want you to have a thriving marriage. A thriving marriage will lead you to the lasting fulfillment and joy that you are looking for.

We talked about the inevitability of change in marriage earlier. The inevitability of change is true of individuals as well. You are not the same husband or wife today that you were when you made your wedding vows. You will not be the same husband or wife ten years from now that you are today. Change is inevitable. Growth is not. You have changed. Has it been for better or worse? You will change. Will it be for better or worse? And will you grow? How?

The reality is that marriage is always two people struggling with sin entering into an intimate relationship built upon trust, love, and commitment. Sin is a common element to all marriages and a challenge with which all couples struggle. Swiss philosopher Denis de Rougemont said, "In as much as when taken one by one most human beings of both sexes are either rogues or neurotics, why should they turn into angels the moment they are paired?"[3]

In one sense de Rougemont is quite right. The simple act of making marriage vows does not guarantee moral growth or character development. But we reject his pessimism. It is possible that "rogues and neurotics" will be unable to overcome their sinful nature and problems will abound in their marriage. Jen has seen this time and again in her practice. You have seen it plastered on television and headlines. Yet, in Christ, God has given us the ability to overcome our roguish and neurotic natures.

Marriage is not about growing in happiness. It is about growing in holiness. Now don't get us wrong. We want you to be happy. If, however, you are going to experience that kind of marriage, you need to accept that the reason to be married isn't to be happy. The reason to be married is to be holy. We honestly believe that if you accept that premise, your marriage will be happier. A thriving marriage that lasts for the rest of your lives will ultimately result in joy.

Yet, we just told you that marriage will not automatically make you holy. How can marriage be about becoming more holy if it doesn't make you holy? That's a very good question. We're glad you asked.

Marriage is a crucible in which our character is formed. As our

---

[3] Denis de Rougemont, *Love in the Western World*, trans. Montgomery Belgion (Princeton, NJ: Princeton Univ. Press, 1956), 300.

character is formed in our marriage, we can become more holy. Every choice we make, whether in our marriage or any other aspect of life, is either drawing us closer to or further away from God. Each decision is making us more or less holy.

In most of the places in which we operate in life, the spiritual ramifications are ignored. Unless you're working in an overtly Christian organization (i.e. church, parachurch, Christian operated business), your boss doesn't care about the spiritual implications of your decisions. Your boss cares that you accomplish the mission of the organization. Your friends, depending on how close they are to you, may care about your spiritual growth. If they do, however, they don't have the access to your life that a spouse does. Friends, moreover, are more easily avoided, ignored, or the relationship ended than a spouse.

Marriage is a context where your character is completely on display. Your home is the place where you retreat from the world and relax. It is the place, more than any other, where you relax and are completely yourself. Your spouse sees you in those relaxed unguarded moments. Good or bad your spouse sees it all.

Your spouse, therefore, is the person most likely to see the areas where you need to grow and is the most capable to help you grow in them. As described above, marriage is the context in which we can experience permanent unconditional love. This unconditional love is necessary for the kind of spiritual growth we all need.

Being corrected is never comfortable. Having your character flaws pointed out to you is probably the worst. The natural human inclination is to presume the worst in our critic. Afterall, we are all the heroes of our own stories. Yet, in the context of permanent love you can trust the critique of the person that promises to love you for better or for worse. You can trust their honest feedback because they want what's best for you. You know they want what's best for you because it is the best for your marriage and therefore the best for them, too.

As Christians, our goal should always be to be more like Jesus every day. Marriage is not about your happiness. It is about your holiness. A reason to be married is to be more godly.

Representing God

In every wedding ceremony that Bryon performs, he talks about the spiritual union that happens between a husband and wife when they get married. The Bible describes it like this, "This explains why a man leaves his father and mother and is joined to his wife, and the two are united into one." (Genesis 2:24 NLT). In the New Testament Jesus says, "But 'God made them male and female' from the beginning of creation. This explains why a man leaves his father and mother and is joined to his wife, and the two are united into one.' Since they are no longer two but one, let no one split apart what God has joined together" (Mark 10:6-9 NLT). Here the Bible is describing a mystical, spiritual reality. When you got married, it was more than merely a social contract set up by human government; indeed, it was set up by God in Genesis, long before societies and human government. God did not design marriage as merely a social construct to maintain civil order, protect women, or determine inheritance rights. God ordained marriage as part of the *imago dei* (image of God).

Now we get it, this sounds like it's a bit much. What does marriage have to do with how we reflect God? Let us explain.

Have you ever thought for a moment that God has never been lonely? Even before God created humans he was never lonely. God has never been lonely because God has never been alone. God eternally exists as a trinity: the Father, the Son, and the Holy Spirit. God eternally exists as three unique persons but one God. These three persons exist eternally united by permanent, unfailing love.

We see this expressed well in the icon created by Russion painter Andrei Rublev in the 15th century, ***The Trinity*** (also called ***The Hospitality of Abraham***). It is his most famous work, the most famous of all Russian icons, and it is regarded as one of the highest achievements of Russian art. *The Trinity* depicts the three angels who visited Abraham at the Oak of Mamre (Genesis 18:1–8), but the painting is full of symbolism and is interpreted as an icon of the Holy Trinity. The three persons of the Holy Trinity are seated in a circular configuration at a table. The poses and the inclinations of the Holy Spirit and the Son's heads demonstrate their submission to the Father, yet their placement on the thrones at the same level symbolizes equality. At the time of Rublev, the Holy Trinity was the embodiment of spiritual unity, peace, harmony, mutual love and humility.[4]

Marriage is intended to reflect this spiritual reality. God exists as three persons yet one God. A marriage is two people yet one couple. The trinity is held together by mutual love between the Father, the Son, and the Holy Spirit. A marriage is held together by mutual love between a husband and a wife. A Christian marriage reflects in part the truth of the triune God.

Yet, what do people see of God when they see a marriage? The first thing people see in a Christian marriage of the truth of God is their love for one another. In John 13:32, Jesus said that others would know we were Christians by our love for one another. It's important to notice what Jesus didn't say. There are a lot of good things Christians do that are not the way people will know we follow Jesus. Jesus did not say how much we give, how often we go to church, how often we serve, how often we read the Bible, how often we tell people about Jesus, how we vote, how we engage in civic activities such as protests or mailing campaigns, or hundreds of other good things that Christians do would be the way people would know we were Christians.

Jesus said people would know we were Christians by how we love each other. The people with whom you come into contact should see God in how you love your spouse. The way you talk to each other reveals your love of each other to others. Your nonverbal communication reveals a lot about your love for each other. How you serve each other reveals your love for each other. Perhaps most importantly, how you talk about your spouse when they are not there reveals a ton about how you love each other. As a Christian couple, how you love each other sends a message to the people around you about God's love.

Once Jen was speaking with a realtor and underwriter regarding the closing on the sale of a home we owned. She expressed that while she understood the legal and financial impacts, she would have to discuss with Bryon before a final decision was reached and announced. Why? Why would a lawyer need to talk to someone else about the legal implications of a contract? Because that was the loving way to treat Bryon. Even the underwriter acknowledged this, saying, "I want you to be my lawyer

---

[4] https://en.wikipedia.org/wiki/Trinity_(Andrei_Rublev)#cite_note-conf-6 accessed May 20, 2020.

because if you treat your husband so well, I know that you'll look out for me and treat me well, too!"

One of God's favorite metaphors for his relationship with us is marriage. The Old Testament is the story of God's unquenchable love for Israel, who consistently rejected God's love and chased after other gods and goals. Through the prophets of the Old Testament, God describes himself as the husband of an unfaithful wife as a metaphor of his relationship with Israel (Jeremiah 2:23-5:15; Ezekiel 16:1-63; Hosea). In the New Testament the metaphor is extended to us, the Christian church. Jesus refers to himself as the bridegroom in a clear metaphor for his relationship to his followers as a husband (Mark 2:19 and parallels). In Revelation, John describes the faithful being revealed as Jesus' bride (Revelation 3:12; 21:2, 9-10). When describing marriage, Paul also makes allusion to Jesus as the husband of the church (Ephesians 5:22-23).

The fact that God so often refers to his relationship with his people as a marriage shows both the importance of marriage as a human relationship in God's view and its importance for revealing God to the world. A Christian couple reveals something about God's love by the way they interact with and love each other.

The way in which you love the people around you also is an indicator of God's love. If you have children, this is particularly true in how you love your children. If you have children, people are watching how you love them. God also consistently reveals himself as a parent in Scripture. Jesus referred to the first person of the trinity as his and our heavenly father. The biblical references to God as the father of his people are almost innumerable.[5] If God reveals himself as a parent then there is something about parenthood that reflects the love of God. People are watching the way you treat your children. The way you love your children shows them something of the love of God.

It does not stop, however, with how you love your children. As a couple, the way you love everyone with whom you come into contact shows others something of God's love. In Matthew 22:37-40 Jesus told those around him what the greatest commandments were. The first is to love

---

[5] If you are interested in doing the research on your own, we recommend *Nave's Topical Bible* as a starting point to identify the passages that discuss the fatherhood of God.

God with everything that you are; and the second, and equally important to Jesus, is to love your neighbor as yourself. Our love for those around us not only reveals something of God's love; it is a command, a demanding imperative to take action to love.

Conclusion

So we'll ask you again, why are you married? There are a lot of reasons to be married. Some are better than others. From a biblical perspective, our experience in counseling couples, as well as our own marriage we think there are three reasons to be married: (1) to experience the mature fulfilling love that God intends for you, (2) grow to be more like Jesus, and (3) represent God to the people around you.

Ultimately, it doesn't really matter what we think. Your marriage is your marriage. You need to decide for yourselves why you're married. Whatever those reasons are, they will affect every decision you make about your marriage. It will affect whether or not you have a thriving marriage.

Action Step:

Before you keep reading this book take some time together and discuss why you're married.

CHAPTER 2

WHY MARRIAGE?

In the last chapter we asked you why you were married. We offered our reasons for why you should be married but the whole conversation begs the question, "why marriage?" We offered reasons to be married and general concepts regarding the purpose of marriage. But let's be honest with each other: for some people knowing the reasons to be married may not be enough to get them through tough times in their marriage.

Hopefully you haven't experienced this in your marriage, but sometimes couples go through periods of unhappiness when they question if it's even worth staying married. Sometimes arguments last so long that they feel irreconcilable. There are times when a friend or coworker seems to understand you better than your spouse. You may one day come home to your spouse and still feel lonely. Life at home on top of work and everything else can sometimes feel overwhelming. There's no guilt or shame in feeling unhappy in your marriage at times. It is important, however, to navigate and manage these feelings well and in a manner that honors God, your spouse, and your marriage.

In later chapters, we offer some skills and insights on how to deal specifically with those feelings, issues, and more. Before we get to that, though, we think it's important to know why using those skills is worth the effort. The why of the end state determines the resources a commander is willing to put into the mission. In this chapter we're going to discuss why having a thriving marriage is worth the effort. We're going to show you why you should bother staying married even if you at times don't feel like it.

The End of the Story

Have you ever noticed that marriage is often the end of the story? In the fairy tales the prince and princess get married and live "happily ever after. The end." In popular culture marriage is often spoken of as the end of life. Once you get married there's no more fun. No more partying. No more sex. Life as you know it ends.

When we were getting married, Bryon heard over and over again that as soon as we were married Jen was going to make him sell his motorcycle. After all, once you get married you have to give up everything fun. Jen actually took personal offense to the comment and was adamant that Bryon not sell the motorcycle.[6] Marriage should not be an end to fun but rather a transition to a new way of experiencing the fun of life.

Marriage is experiencing the fun of life together with your spouse. What is the first thing you want to do when you have a great experience? Usually, the impulse is to share it. Don't pretend that's not you. Look at your Instagram or Facebook and tell us we're wrong. When you're married you always have someone to share the fun with.

Here is the problem that we have observed: Marriage is not viewed as a life expanding experience. It is viewed as a life limiting experience. In the United States there is a huge value on the ability to choose. American culture has, moreover, been afflicted with a severe case of what we'll call *FOMOitis*. You know what we're talking about. Americans have a very strong Fear Of Missing Out. Living in a college town we hear about this a lot. People do not want to commit to plans because something better might come along. Or, people will jump on a perceived opportunity that has a limited timeframe because they're afraid they'll miss out on it otherwise.

FOMOitis can be particularly dangerous with regard to marriage. Everytime we make a choice to do something, we are choosing not to do

---

[6] Full disclosure from Bryon: I did eventually sell my motorcycle but it was not because Jen and I got married. I sold it after our daughter, Brenda, was born, over Jen's protests to keep it. I had a choice to make. I could either spend time riding my motorcycle or spend time with my daughter. I couldn't do both. Spending time with my little girl has always been more fun than riding a motorcycle. She's big enough to ride with me now and so is our son, so now I take them on motorcycle rides on the motorcycle that I inherited from my dad.

a myriad of other things that could have been done. For instance; our son Jonathan is a huge fan of the band Imagine Dragons. He has been a fan since he was two years old and used to sing himself to sleep singing their song *Radioactive*. By the way, there's not much cuter than listening to a toddler sing:

I'm waking up.
I feel it in my bones.
Enough to make my sister *blow.*

Like many of us he doesn't always hear the lyrics correctly.

Anyway, in the summer of 2018 we wanted to do something fun with him so we decided to get tickets to see (and meet!) Imagine Dragons. His sister isn't a fan so she decided to spend the night at a friend's house. There are a lot of other things we could have done. We missed out on a leisurely night of watching TV then going to bed at a reasonable hour. We missed out on seeing a movie that night. We missed out on the opportunity to use that money to buy something for the house. We missed out on everything that we would/could have done with our time and money instead of going to the Imagine Dragons concert. It was a great evening, but we know that choice by its very nature is limiting.

When you said "I do" at the altar, you said "I don't" to every other potential spouse. You missed out on all the opportunities that those potential spouses have to offer. The culture of *FOMOitis* argues that it's not worth it. There are too many experiences you won't have. Besides, you can live together without getting married and receive all the benefits of marriage without any of the sacrifices. Marriage once intended to be a permanent union for "mutual love, procreation and protection" has become a "terminal sexual contract" intended to meet individual physical desires.[7] Of course if this is true, why bother? There are plenty of other ways to gratify physical desires.

We naturally think this *FOMOitis* is ridiculous and will explain below but there's another false view of marriage equally pernicious as *FOMOitis*

---

[7] John Witte Jr., *From Sacrament to Contract: Marriage, Religion, and Law in the Western Tradition* (Louisville: John Knox Press, 1997), 209.

but less in your face. This false view of marriage leads to many marriages failing. We will call it <u>forbidden love</u>.

Denis de Rougemont traced this false view back to medieval troubadours in the twelfth century.[8] In his work he observed a trend in western literature. A majority of the romantic stories western culture tells itself idealize love for one who is unavailable. *Romeo and Juliet* is an example that is repeated over and over again. The love of two young people from different worlds is glamourized as somehow purer than conventional romances in those cultures. This love denied speaks deeply into western culture and is repeated time and again. It is such an integral part of American culture, it was used in the blockbuster 1996 film *Titanic* (Jack and Rose) and more recently used in *Avengers: Infinity War* in the opening scenes with Vision and the Scarlet Witch.

Another popular version of this is the love between Guinevere and Lancelot in the stories of King Arthur. In these stories two people love each other but that love is denied because one of them is bound, usually in marriage, to another person. You're meant to feel sorry for the lovers for whom love is denied because theirs is considered the stronger purer love. Hundreds of books, movies, plays, and TV shows either retell or are inspired by the Arthurian legend. The two key events that are almost always included are Arthur retrieving the sword from the stone and the forbidden love between Guinevere and Lancelot.

Forbidden or denied love has become a significant aspect of western culture. The narrative of culture says that love denied or impeded is better (and somehow purer!) than love consumated through socially acceptable means, i.e. marriage. This narrative leads people to believe that romance outside of marriage is better than that within. Forbidden fruit is somehow sweeter than the fruit that belongs to you, at least according to that narrative.

In the real world, this narrative never works out. The news is full of stories of wealthy people pursuing co-workers and employees that are not their spouse. Jen and I have personal experience with friends having affairs. In television, movies, and literature, these relationships usually work out for the better for the protagonists of the story. In real life, that is not the real story.

---

[8] *Love in the Western World*

The Real Story

Here is the reality. You have been affected by those false narratives we discussed above. We all have. It's just like the frog in the pot metaphor.[9] We don't realize how much these false views of love and marriage affect us because it's too pervasive for us to even see. The sad truth is that we've seen these false narratives ruin marriages time and time again. The only way to overcome them is to change your perspective by focusing on the truth that is counter to these false narratives. Just as Paul says in Romans 12:2, "Do not conform to the pattern of this world, but be transformed by the renewing of your mind."[10] You renew your mind by focusing on the truth and letting the truth inform and then correct your false beliefs.

Now, let's start with the idea that marriage is the end of the story. Could anything be more ridiculous? First, why are there so many married people in the world if marriage is the end of everything? If marriage was really such a bad thing, no amount of social pressure would keep the antiquated institution alive. There is nothing, especially in western culture, demanding that marriage continue. Still people, from all cultures, socio-economic statuses, and religions want to get married. Despite the cultural jokes, sex does not stop once people get married. If that were the case there would be no families with children. Fun does not stop at the altar.

While the false view of marriage says that it is the end of happiness and fun, the evidence tells quite a different story. Psychology has observed that

---

[9] The frog in the pot is a common metaphor explaining how it is hard for us to be aware of the influence our environment has on us. If you put a frog in a pot of boiling water, it will jump out immediately because it feels the heat. If you put a frog in a pot of cold water then set it on the stove and slowly heat the water, the frog will stay in the pot and slowly allow itself to be cooked. This is because frogs are cold-blooded and will not notice the water getting hotter because their body temperature is rising at the same rate as their environment. In the same way, we do not notice the influence culture has on us because we tend to change with our culture.

OK, what kind of sick person would do this to a poor unsuspecting frog? Let us say now that we do not condone such behavior. Modern biologists, moreover, say this is not true. At some point the frog will still jump out. This, however, is a metaphor so let's not read too much into it and accept the reality that culture affects how we think.

[10] Unless otherwise indicated, Bible references are taken from the New English Translation.

the quality of one's relationships is directly correlated with their happiness. Marriage is uniquely capable of building happiness because of the nature of the relationship.[11]

> The National Opinion Research Center, in Chicago, Illinois surveyed 35,000 Americans over a thirty years period. 40% of married people said they were "very happy" while only 24% of unmarried, divorced, separated, and widowed people said this. The happiness advantage for marrieds holds true when you examine the results considering age, income, and gender.[12]

In fact, a cursory review of studies will reveal that marriage is highly correlated with happiness. To be fair, it is hard to say if marriage makes people happy or happy people get and stay married. The most important thing to observe from the research, however, is that the popular consensus that marriage is the end of happiness is patently false. Research shows that at the least, marriage creates a fertile ground for happiness to grow and may even be a significant cause of happiness.

OK, But Why Marriage?

Alright, we've made the point that marriage is not the end of happiness, but we still haven't answered the question, why marriage? Can't other things provide fulfillment and happiness? Isn't Jesus the ultimate source of happiness and fulfilment? Why does God care about marriage anyway?

At this point we won't spend a lot of time going through all of the biblical passages that describe God's great care and concern for marriage. We're presuming you are somewhat familiar with them. If not, take a break and do a quick Google search for "marriage and Bible." You'll get a good summary.

Instead, let's look at the first marriage and see what God said in that

---

[11] LInda and Charlie Bloom, "Marriage and Happiness: A Direct Path to Happiness", *Psychology Today*, https://www.psychologytoday.com/us/blog/stronger-the-broken-places/201802/marriage-and-happiness, accessed 4 Sep 2018.
[12] ibid.

moment. We draw your attention here first because it's incredible how much you learn about people and the uniqueness of marriage in chapter 2 of Genesis.

The first thing you notice reading the account of the creation of humanity in Genesis 2 is that humans are unique among creation. God "breathed into his nostrils the breath of life" (Genesis 2:7b). Into no other creature did God breathe the breath of life. So, when God created the first human he blew his own breath into him and only then did "the man become a living being" (Genesis 2:7c).

Ok, let's break this down. God is spirit (John 4:24). He doesn't need to breathe. He, moreover, didn't need to breathe into a clay model to make a living being. He had already made plenty of living things just by speaking them into existence. So, what is going on here? This speaks to the uniqueness of humanity among creation. Humans are unique among creation because they are the only thing in creation that is both physical and spiritual. When God breathed the breath of life into the first human, he imparted something of himself into the person. He gave him a spirit. He made the man in his own image having a characteristic of God that no other creature had. This spirit is what gives humanity a conscience. It gives us all a sense of morality. This spiritual nature of humanity is also significant for marriage.

The fact that humans are different from the animals is one reason marriage is different from the pairing practices of other animals. There are other creatures that mate for life which may look similar to human marriage. To compare animals that mate for life with human marriage, however, is a false equivalency. From the beginning, humans were different from animals. Human relationships are, therefore, different. Marriage is different from anything in the animal kingdom. Human marriage is spiritual and physical.

Now jump ahead to verse 18 where God says, "It is not good for the man to be alone" (Genesis 2:18a). This should stand out to you because it is the first time in history that something was labeled as "not good." That's not an exaggeration. Up to this point everything in the universe had been declared by God as good or very good. Before this point, nothing had ever been not good. And what is not good? It is not good that the man is alone.

That's huge! Of all the things that could have not been good, the thing that was not good was that the first human was alone.

Some theologians argue that the reason this is not good has to do with the command to "be fruitful and multiply" (Genesis 1:28). This, perhaps, makes logical sense. The man could not multiply by himself; rather, more is needed for procreation.

We don't think that solution fits the structure of Genesis or the context in which the passage is written. Starting in verse 5 of chapter 2, Genesis is an elaboration on the uniqueness of humanity in creation and a prelude to what will happen in chapter 3 when sin enters the world through the sin of our first parents, Adam and Eve. The theme is that humans are unique because of their spirituality. All humans are both material and spiritual beings. The fact that it is "not good" that the man is alone must be tied to what was revealed about man: his uniqueness in creation.

It is, therefore, not good that the man is alone because he is like God in that he is spirit. We say that man is spirit rather than saying man has a spirit because humanity is unique in all of creation in this way. Humans are both spirit and body. Nothing else in all of creation is both spiritual and material. The angels and demons are purely spiritual. Animals are purely physical. God did not breathe his breath of life into them. Humans are not spirits in bodies. Nor are human beings bodies that have spirits. Humans are spirits and bodies combined completely. That is why the ultimate fulfillment of God's plan is both body *and* spirit resurrection on a new earth not existing eternally as spirits in heaven (c.f. Revelation 21-22)[13].

The spirit given to humans by God is something of the essence of God. It is an aspect of the image of God. Since humans are created in the image of a communal God they require community to fully experience being human. Looking at this through New Testament eyes, it is even clearer. The New Testament reveals more concretely that God has eternally existed as the Trinity. The triune godhead has never been alone. God is and has always been a communal God. God has always existed in perfect love and community. Humanity, created in the image of God, with the breath of

---

[13] This is also why it is so important to note that at the incarnation, Jesus became fully human while staying fully God. Jesus shared in every aspect of our nature with the exception of sin.

God making them spiritual beings, has always been meant to live in a loving community. It was, therefore, not good when the man was alone.[14]

At this point, the man did not know that it was not good that he was alone. Let's face it, he didn't know much of anything at this point. God revealed the truth of the matter to him by giving him a task. He was to name all the animals.

> The Lord God formed out of the ground every living animal of the field and every bird of the air. He brought them to the man to see what he would name them, and whatever the man called each living creature, that was its name. So the man named all the animals, the birds of the air, and the living creatures of the field, but for Adam no companion who corresponded to him was found (Genesis 2:19-20).

This task was a huge blessing for Adam and Eve. Adam would never have realized the depth of his need for companionship if God had merely provided him with Eve. The experience of seeing all the animals and seeing that among all creation he was unique showed Adam that it was not good that he was alone. Scripture does not reveal what Adam thought or felt throughout this process. We imagine that it was incredibly eye-opening for him. During this experience, Adam must have, for the first time, felt very much alone compared with the rest of creation. For the first time, Adam felt something was not good.

Think of how similar this is to the time before you met your spouse. How did your experiences before you were married prepare you for the

---

[14] We want to recognize at this point that singleness is not an inherently bad thing. Community exists in many forms other than marriage. Marriage is, however, a unique form of community with a unique place in creation and human society. There, clearly, is nothing wrong with being single. Neither Jesus nor Paul married and this did not make them less human. Jesus himself honors singleness in Matthew 19:12 when he said "For there are some eunuchs who were that way from birth, and some who were made eunuchs by others, and some who became eunuchs for the sake of the kingdom of heaven. The one who is able to accept this should accept it." Much more could be said on the high value of singleness but this is a marriage book so we will not be discussing it further here.

unique relationship that is marriage? God uses our time before marriage to prepare us for marriage and to help us appreciate the relationship and value our life partner brings into our lives.

After Adam learned that it was not good that he was alone, God created a "companion for him who corresponds to him" (Genesis 2:18b). The word translated as "companion" here is often translated as "helper" (ESV, NIV, NLT) or the King James Version says, "help meet" (whatever that means). What we'll say here is that the word was never intended to communicate lower status or subservience. In fact, in the Bible, frequently the same root word refers to God.

We like to think of "helper" in this context similar to a partnership in a law practice. Each partner in the practice is equal. Yes, we acknowledge there are levels of partnership in some firms.[15] Let's keep this simple for the sake of the illustration and presume that this law firm is not large enough to have varying levels of partnership. Here, the partners are equal. No partner has authority over the other. Instead, they work together with the mutual goal of running the firm. Each partner has different responsibilities and brings different skills to the partnership. Perhaps one specializes in bankruptcy and the other specializes in criminal defense. The firm would not run as well if one of the partners was not there and could likely not handle these areas of expertise with the same competence and skill. This is just like marriage. Each spouse brings something into the marriage necessary for the marriage to be all that it is intended to be.

Now let's look at the word that is more relevant for our current conversation. The companion that God made *corresponded* to the man (Genesis 2:18).[16] What does that mean? It could simply mean female. If the passage was limited to the command to be fruitful and multiply, then this would be the best answer. As was shown above, however, that is not the intent of the passage. Eve's correspondence to Adam goes much deeper than the biological necessity to facilitate procreation.

---

[15] There can be varying levels of partnership based on funds contributed, years of experience, and merit. If we talk about smaller law firms, partners are often equals but can have differing specializations in practice. The partners can help with the other's cases and appear on behalf of the clients in all cases.

[16] Some translations say "fit for" (ESV) or "suitable for" (NASB, NIV). We prefer corresponding to because it seems to communicate the intent of the passage better.

The translation notes in the New English Translation help a lot. They say:

> The Hebrew expression כְּנֶגְדּוֹ (*kénegdo*) literally means "according to the opposite of him." Translations such as "suitable [for]" (NASB, NIV), "matching," "corresponding to" all capture the idea. ... The man's form and nature are matched by the woman's as she reflects him and complements him. Together they correspond. In short, this prepositional phrase indicates that she has everything that God had invested in him.[17]

In other words, God made the right kind of companion that the man needed to correct the problem: he was alone. The woman was the solution to the problem because she was equally unique in creation. Like the man, she was created in the image of God (Genesis 1:26-27). Since she was "taken out of man" (Genesis 2:23), we know that she was a physical body who also had the breath of God in her. She too was spirit. In all the ways that the man was unique in creation so was the woman. She was the companion that corresponded to him and thus was able to solve the problem that it was not good that the man be alone.

Later in chapter 2 the man and the woman are married. In the next chapter, we look at those passages to explain the true nature of marriage.

Conclusion

Ok, we've written a lot and this chapter is more technical than most because we have gone pretty deep theologically. We should probably bring this in for a landing. In the last chapter we talked about why you should stay married. We said that a thriving marriage helps you experience the mature fulfilling love that God intends for you, to grow to be more like Jesus, and represent God to the people around you. We opened this chapter with the question, "why marriage?" Is marriage really the best way to fulfill

---

[17] Biblical Studies Press, (2005) *The NET Bible First Edition; Bible. English. NET Bible.; The NET Bible*, accessed Jul 15, 2020.

those goals? Couldn't other relationships do a better job without all the negative baggage of marriage?

If you limit your understanding of marriage to the false narrative that it is the end of love and fun, then marriage probably isn't the best way to fulfill these goals listed above. Yet, that narrative is false. Research, statistics, and our experience talking to and observing couples over the last 20 years or so has proven that narrative false.

Humans need companions that correspond to them because they were created for intimate community like the triune God. Humans created male and female are unique in creation because we are created in the image of God. Our first parents, Adam and Eve, had something of God breathed into them the moment they were created. Two people bonded together by God are able to uniquely experience the love of God, become more like Jesus, and express God to the world.

Action Step:

Tonight before you go to bed, take a moment to discuss with your spouse how you best express God to the world as individuals and also as a married couple.

CHAPTER 3

WHAT IS MARRIAGE?

In the past two chapters, we talked about why you are married and why marriage is so important. Unfortunately, we all see marriages ending at an astounding rate. At the time we are writing this, approximately 40% - 50% of first marriages end in divorce and subsequent marriages end in divorce at an even higher rate.

In Jen's legal practice, Bryon's experience in the military, and our shared experiences in ministry, we have found that most of the marriages that end start developing problems much, much earlier than the decision to divorce. Often the problems start a decade or more before the couple starts seriously considering divorce. Many of the problems actually start quite early in the marriage. Most start within the first 3 - 5 years.

While the probability of marriage ending is high and the roots of the problem run deep and start early, we believe that two people devoted to each other, their marriage, and God can have a thriving, marriage that will last a lifetime. That's why we're writing this book. We hope that as you continue to read, you will develop the skills to identify and address problems in your marriage early so that they do not fester and later lead to divorce.

Up to this point we've established much of the context in which *Operation: Thriving Marriage* operates. We've laid down the why of the operation. We still need to establish the what. We need to define thriving marriage. To do that, we will start by defining marriage. Once we know what marriage is, then we can figure out how to make it thrive.

Marriage Isn't a Contract

According to the Merriam-Webster Dictionary marriage is, "the state of being united as spouses in a consensual and contractual relationship recognized by law."[18] Dictionary.com's definition is a little more expansive, "any of the diverse forms of interpersonal union established in various parts of the world to form a familial bond that is recognized legally, religiously, or socially, granting the participating partners mutual conjugal rights and responsibilities."[19]

The legality of marriage is still somewhat significant in America. America continues to value marriage as an institution legally and grants certain rights to those who are married, even if marriage is losing significance socially. From a legal perspective, then, marriage is a contract. It is an agreement between two parties that grants them certain legal rights. In that way, it is similar to buying into a business or signing a lease. Two or more parties have a recognized agreement that grants them certain legal rights.

Is a Christian marriage something more? I have heard many sermons describing how Christian marriage is a covenant not a contract. A covenant is something very different from a contract. In the sermons, a covenant is different in two ways. First, a covenant is different because one of the parties involved is God. A marriage involves three parties: husband, wife, and God. Second, contracts by their nature are breakable. Contracts can be broken. There are consequences to a broken contract, often financial, but they can be broken. A covenant cannot be broken because God is a party to the agreement, and he is eternal.

That's a great sermon. It preaches well. Unfortunately, it's not accurate. Like the societal contract, it still presents marriage as something that is transactional. All that sermon does is raise the stakes of the contract. We've heard it all too many times and also seen marriages officiated with that sermon succumb to divorce again and again.

True biblical marriage fundamentally differs from contracts and covenants. When two people are married they are fundamentally changed forever. Instead of being individuals bound in an agreement,

---

[18] https://www.merriam-webster.com/dictionary/marriage accessed Oct. 3, 2018
[19] https://www.dictionary.com/browse/marriage?s=t accessed Oct. 3, 2018

two individuals, while maintaining individuality, become one. This truth far surpasses a contract or transaction; rather, marriage is a God-ordained joining of two individuals into one couple for life.

A Short Biblical Theology of Marriage

To understand what marriage is, we have to start again at the first marriage between Adam and Eve. What happens when two people are married? According to Scripture, "a man leaves his father and mother and is united to his wife, and they become one flesh" (Genesis 2:24 NIV). Notice the three things that happen when two people are married:

1. They leave their first family.
2. They are united to each other.
3. They become one flesh.

On the next few pages, we'll look at each of these in turn.

Leaving Your First Family

The first thing that happens in marriage is that you leave your first family. You separate from your parents. Now some will say they left their family a long time before they got married. In America, the average age for getting married is late twenties[20] and many of our peers have married in their thirties. As such, many young adults live on their own and not with family for years before they marry.

Many people physically leave their parents' home long before they're married. They may go away to college and graduate school. They may take a job in another city away from their parents and siblings. They don't, however, leave their parents emotionally or spiritually.

Think about it. If you moved out of your parents house before you were married, who was your family? With the exception of escaping abuse or other unhealthy family situations, we have never met an unmarried

---

[20] https://www.dailydot.com/irl/average-age-marriage-by-state/ accessed Jul. 2, 2020.

individual that did not still consider themselves a part of their family of origin (the family that they were born into, or that raised you in cases of adoption and fostering). The emotional and spiritual ties to their parents and siblings are still strong.

Once a person is married, those bonds change. They were not eliminated. They were, however, changed. The family to which you belong primarily is now the family you have created with your spouse.

This does not mean that your family of origin is no longer important. It does not mean that you no longer love them. It means that your emotional and spiritual bond, in healthy marriages, should be stronger now with your spouse than with the family you grew up in. No longer are your parents and siblings the people who are your primary physical, emotional, or spiritual support. That role rightfully belongs to your spouse.

Of course, your first family still can provide physical, emotional, and spiritual support. And we hope they do! Anytime Bryon is facing a significant decision that baffles him, his habit was to call his dad. While he was living, Bryon's dad was one of the wise counselors Bryon sought. Jen, however, is, and was, Bryon's primary counselor, since we got married. She is his primary physical, emotional, and spiritual support. Since Bryon's dad passed away, he calls his mom almost every day. That call is somewhat of an anchor for him. He still gets emotional support from his mom. It is simply different now that we're married.

For most people, leaving their family of origin is a process. There are habits and relationships that have literally formed throughout your lifetime. For some of you it took or is taking a conscious effort to separate from your parents (while hopefully still maintaining strong and healthy ties to them!). This is, however, something you need to put conscious effort towards.

Communication is one of the significant causes of unhealthy marriages. When your family of origin is your primary physical, emotional and spiritual support, you're communicating with them in a way that you should be communicating with your spouse and also placing your spouse in a lesser role. When that happens, spouses feel disconnected and devalued. You must include your spouse and value your relationship with them above the relationship you have with your parents and siblings.

If you are realizing that you still need to leave your parents, here are a couple of steps you can take to help.

- The next time you want advice from your parents, ask your spouse for advice first.
- If the advice you are usually getting from your parents involves your relationship with your spouse, take some time to discuss your relationship concerns with your spouse and come up with an action plan together.
- Go on a parent-advice fast. Don't call your parents for advice for a week or a month; but be in touch about other things. Experience life without your parents' advice for a while. (If you choose to do this, make sure you tell your parents what's going on. You still love them after all.)

If, on the other hand, you are realizing that your partner is the one that has not yet separated from their first family, take some time to discuss this section with your spouse. Share specifics with them. Tell your spouse how you feel. Discuss a plan on how you can build your relationship and be your spouse's primary physical, emotional, and spiritual support.

It's important to realize that you may have done something in the past that signaled that you could not or would not be the support they need. You are going to have to work hard on being the support they need so they have the trust in you to be able to leave their first family. Do not expect immediate results. This is a process. Together you will become stronger if you are willing to put the effort into becoming the physical, emotional, and spiritual support that your spouse needs and take the risk to trust your spouse to be the physical, emotional, and spiritual support that you need.

United to Each Other

This is the most visible aspect of marriage. The word used here is the Hebrew word דָּבַק (*dabaq*). The basic definition of *dabaq* is to stick to or join together. In the Old Testament, it often describes how your own body parts stick together or are joined together.

In the context of marriage, however, the sense of *dabaq* is a little different. In this sense, *dabaq* would be better defined as, to cling to out of loyalty. The same word is used to describe how Ruth clung to her mother-in-law and followed her back to Israel after Ruth's husband died (Ruth 1:14). It is also used to describe the loyalty of David's soldiers (2 Samuel 20:2).

Doesn't sound very romantic does it? At first blush clinging out of loyalty doesn't inspire much passion. We even view "clingy" people as annoying.

Ok, but step back for a minute and look at what's going on here. In truth, loyal devotion is sexy. When you know that your partner is fiercely loyal and dedicated to you and your relationship, that can be quite a turn on. The fact is, everyone wants to know where they stand in relationships. In marriage, we all want loyalty, fidelity, and trust. *Dabaq* is a passion inducing reality in marriage.

Once married, two people become one couple. The Hebrew construction implies something greater than a one time event. It is rather an event that continues indefinitely.

Think of it in the context of breathing. You don't breathe once in your life then you're good. Breathing is a continuous act.

When our children were born the experiences were very different, as it is for everyone. Our oldest, Brenda, started screaming as soon as she was born. During the next hour, as Bryon held our baby girl in his arms, she screamed "oooohlaah! oooohlaah! oooohlah!"

Jonathan, on the other hand, was unimpressed by the whole birth experience. He was born and was completely silent. The nurses reassured us that every indication was that he was healthy. His pulse was strong. He just didn't want to scream. Now, of course, a newborn screaming is important to clear out the gunk in their lungs. So, the nurses started blowing air in his face from the oxygen tube next to Jen's bed to make him mad enough to scream. After a minute or so, he started screaming.

Here's the point: both our children, like every other living person in the world, took their first breath, but they didn't stop breathing. We all consistently breathe. A wedding, like a birth, is one moment in time. The marriage, like breathing, is a continuous and consistent process of becoming one. A process intended to last throughout the rest of your lives.

Here's another example. Being united in marriage is not like being glued together but rather like holding hands. When two things are glued together, it takes no effort to stay together. They are bonded. Being married is more like holding hands. It takes a little effort.

As we said before, we are continuing to write this book during the COVID-19 pandemic. For months we have had to stay home and keep separate from other people so that we are all safe from the virus. During this time, instead of our usual weekly dates, we have taken daily walks to have alone time and stay connected. As we walk through our neighborhood, we hold hands. When two people hold hands, it takes effort to continue holding hands. Not a lot of effort, but effort nonetheless. If one person relaxes, the other can keep the handhold but it takes more effort. If both people relax, the handhold ends. And at any point in time, one person can pull their hand out breaking the handhold.

Are you still loyally clinging to your spouse? Are you daily making an effort to stay connected? Are you still holding hands or have you relaxed your grip?

Being joined together is not a passive reality. To remain joined together requires that you both put forth effort to stay bonded. Don't let go. Your marriage is worth it.

Becoming One Flesh

In our opinion, becoming one flesh is the most misunderstood aspect of a marriage. Many pastors and premarital counseling books focus on sex at this point. In fact, the book we used when we went through premarital counseling said that this referred exclusively to sex. That book argued that the point of this phrase is that sex is only appropriate after marriage. While we agree that sex is for marriage only, there are other passages that communicate that point much better than this passage in Genesis.[21] This verse is, rather, referring to a new spiritual reality you experience when you become married. Theologian Wayne Grudem in his systematic theology

---

[21] If you're interested in reading more about the Bible's negative view on premarital sex, do a word study on fornication. When you read those passages remember that fornication refers to any sexual activity outside the sanctity of marriage.

says, "This unity is not only a physical unity; it is also a spiritual and emotional unity of profound dimensions."[22]

Part of the confusion is the translation of the word "flesh." Today most Christians think of humans as made of two parts; body and soul, or three parts; body, soul, and spirit. This would be a foreign concept to early Hebrews. Early Hebrews viewed humans as a united indivisible whole. Flesh, in this context therefore, refers to the totality of the person. Becoming one flesh then means much more than having sex. Becoming one flesh, rather, refers to the totality of two people becoming one.

There is something sacramental about marriage. Clearly, becoming one flesh does not mean that the two people getting married cease to exist independently in a physical sense. At some esoteric level, however, they do cease to exist independently. Bryon makes this point every time he officiates a wedding. As a Trinity, God has eternally existed as Father, Son, and Holy Spirit. Three persons yet one God. Although we will never fully understand God as three in one, in marriage we are able to experience something of the eternal relationship of God. Through marriage, two individuals created in the image of God become one couple. In marriage, God provides us with a way to experience oneness in community and reflect him to the world around us.

This should impact how you view yourself, your partner, and your marriage. While you do not cease to be individuals, as a couple you are so much more. Nothing you do affects you alone. Everything you do affects both of you and your marriage. Paul says it like this in Ephesians, "In the same way husbands ought to love their wives as their own bodies. He who loves his wife loves himself. For no one has ever hated his own body but he feeds it and takes care of it" (Ephesians 5:28-29a). Once you're married you cannot think of your own interests alone. You must think of and prioritize the interests of your spouse as well. Together you must prioritize your marriage.

Recently when discussing this with a couple for whom we were providing premarital coaching, the groom responded negatively to this idea. In his mind it was both impossible and ridiculous. We all have

---

[22] Wayne A. Grudem and Gregg Allison, *Systematic Theology/Historical Theology Bundle*, (Grand Rapids, MI: Zondervan, 2004), Kindle Edition, Kindle Locations 12382-12383.

individual needs that do not cease to exist once we're married. These needs are physical, psychological, and spiritual. He argued that it is perfectly reasonable to expect these needs to be met.

We agree that individual needs continue once you're married and it is reasonable to expect that they will be met. The issue is focus. If you both are focusing on getting from your partner then it will ultimately pull you apart. If you both are focusing on meeting your partner's needs then it will push you together. How do you want to experience your marriage? Will you together choose to push together or pull apart?

Where is your focus? Do your thoughts and actions reflect that the two of you have become one flesh? Or, are you still living like you are individuals?

You can change course if need be!

As we said at the beginning of this section, this is probably the most important and most misunderstood reality of marriage. Whether you acknowledge it or not, you became one flesh when you got married. If this is an area where you need to focus, here are a couple of suggestions:

- Take a personal inventory. Write down the decisions you made in the past two or three days. Annotate the decisions that reflect an individual focus and the ones that reflect a "one flesh" focus. For the decisions that reflect only an individual focus, write down ideas of how you could have had a "one flesh" focus.
- Find someplace where you can be alone together without distractions. Take turns sharing when you have felt most like "one flesh" and when you have felt the least like "one flesh."

A Note About Sex, Uniting, and One Flesh

We mentioned earlier that becoming one flesh is not only about sex. While that is true, we should note that sex is an important component of becoming one flesh. Having sex with your spouse helps to facilitate becoming one flesh and uniting to each other.

One of the biological functions of sex is to bond to people together. When you have sex, the hormone oxytocin is released. Oxytocin is sometimes called the "love hormone" because of its role in bonding two people together. Your body is preprogrammed to bond with the person with whom you have sex. Having sex is not becoming one flesh, but it does bond two people together in a way intended to help them to become one flesh. This is why the Bible consistently prohibits premarital and extramarital sex.

This is the crux of Paul's argument against sexual immorality in 1 Corinthians 6. A common practice in Greek and Roman religions was to have sex with temple prostitutes in worship of their gods. It appears that the church in Corinth had not totally given up the practice, although the church should have been worshiping Jesus alone. In response, Paul wrote:

> The body, however, is not meant for sexual immorality but for the Lord, and the Lord for the body. By his power God raised the Lord from the dead, and he will raise us also. Do you not know that your bodies are members of Christ himself? Shall I then take the members of Christ and unite them with a prostitute? Never! Do you not know that he who unites himself with a prostitute is one with her in body? For it is said, "The two will become one flesh." But whoever is united with the Lord is one with him in spirit.

> Flee from sexual immorality. All other sins a person commits are outside the body, but whoever sins sexually, sins against their own body. Do you not know that your bodies are temples of the Holy Spirit, who is in you, whom you have received from God? You are not your own; you were bought at a price. Therefore honor God with your bodies. (1 Corinthians 6:13b-20 NIV)

Contrary to the character Samantha's musings in the TV show "Sex and the City," sex is never "just sex." Yes, it is a biological drive. But no, it is not something to be taken lightly or casually. Biologically and spiritually, sex bonds two people together. It is a part of how two people, when married, become one flesh.

Conclusion

Fundamental to building a thriving marriage is a firm understanding of the nature of marriage. Marriage is not merely a contractual agreement between two people that can be ended with a clean break and without consequences by one or both parties. Nor is marriage a covenantal agreement between two people and God requiring God's approval to end it. Marriage is a fundamental transformation to the identity of two individuals by which they become one couple and a new family.

A healthy marriage requires that both individuals re-prioritize their lives around each other and their marriage. Once married, your decisions and actions no longer affect you alone; similarly, your spouse's decisions no longer affect your spouse alone. Every decision and action affects you as a couple because you are one. It is also now your responsibility together to grow in unity throughout your lifetimes.

Action steps:

- Discuss with your spouse how each of you have viewed the concept of "one flesh." Has it changed?
- What decisions do you need to make as a couple rather than as separate individuals?

CHAPTER 4

THE GOAL OF MARRIAGE

Marriage has a great capacity for happiness. Having a person share your laughter, your tears, your successes, your failures, your dreams, your fears, and your most intimate thoughts is one of the most fulfilling experiences you will ever have in life. We are created in the image of a relational God. We, therefore, are by nature relational. A companion on life's journey undoubtedly improves our capacity to experience happiness in life.

Here's the thing though: God cares more about your holiness than your happiness. You were not put on this earth primarily to be happy. Creation exists to glorify God. That includes you. You were created primarily to glorify God. The Westminster Catechism says it like this, "Man's chief end is to glorify God and enjoy him forever."

As that is the purpose of humanity, it stands to reason that marriage would support this end. Marriage then is a means by which two people are better able to glorify God and enjoy him. Holiness rather than happiness is required to glorify God because only godly living truly glorifies him. Moreover, happiness is fleeting and often beyond your control. If your goal in life is to be happy, you are doomed to disappointment.

Happiness is Never Permanent

To a great extent, American culture is built on the pursuit of happiness. It is literally written into the foundation of our society. The second paragraph of the Declaration of Independence states, "We hold these truths to be self-evident, that all men are created equal, that they are endowed by their Creator with certain unalienable Rights, that among these are Life, Liberty, and the *Pursuit of Happiness*" (emphasis added). A pursuit of happiness, in and of itself, is not necessarily a bad thing. Happiness is objectively good. The pursuit of happiness, however, is a poor ultimate goal.

Happiness is a poor ultimate goal because it is impossible to maintain. The factors that determine happiness are not all within an individual's control. Take a moment and think about some of the things that make you happy. There are many things that make us happy. Chocolate chip cookies are something that make us happy. We almost always have homemade chocolate chip cookies in the house. Almost every night after the kids go to bed we each get a chocolate chip cookie and a glass of milk. On rare occasions, the cookies get burnt. Now since both of us bake cookies either one of us could be responsible for burning them. It doesn't really matter which one burns them. The happiness of both of us is reduced. For one of us, that is through no fault of our own.

Now that may be a silly example, but you get the point. Happiness is a poor ultimate goal because there are factors contributing to our happiness that we cannot control. Another reason that happiness is a poor ultimate goal is because it is impossible to maintain. God created us to be incredibly adaptable. There is almost no situation to which we cannot adapt.

As a military member, Bryon is very interested in military history. Bryon has read a few books and articles about the experiences of prisoners of war and has even had the privilege of meeting a couple of them. It is amazing how a person can adapt and thrive in some of the most horrendous situations imaginable. There are some great stories of how those heroes overcame their context and ultimately made it home.

The point here, however, is that they did adapt. They overcame because they were able to adapt to horrendous conditions. Just as those prisoners adapted to the horrible conditions of imprisonment, you will adapt to happiness. What makes you happy today won't make you happy a week from now if it stays constant. Just as you don't notice the feel of the clothes touching your skin a few minutes after you put them on, the situation that makes you happy will go unnoticed after a time if it doesn't change. It is one of the ways we adapt to changing situations.

Two of Jen's best friends no longer live in Michigan. One lives in Ohio while the other lives in Florida. One year, Bryon worked with Jen's friends to have them come to Michigan and surprise her for her birthday. Jen was ecstatic when she saw her friends. Jen is very exuberant and almost crushed her friend from Florida with a bear hug when she saw her. Jen was incredibly happy to see them and spend time with them.

If her friends never left, Jen's happiness would have waned. If they moved in and Jen saw them everyday her happiness level would eventually diminish. The uniqueness of the situation was a necessary component of Jen's happiness. Had there been no change in her daily life, there would have been no change in her experience of happiness. Happiness requires change. Happiness is, therefore, virtually impossible to maintain, making happiness a poor ultimate goal.

Many people argue that the goal of marriage is happiness. But, that's simply not true. Marriage is intended to be a permanent union between husband and wife. Happiness, in any relationship or circumstance, is fleeting. A fleeting temporary experience can never be the goal of a permanent lifelong experience.

The Real Goal of Marriage

If the goal of marriage is not happiness, what then is the goal of marriage? To an extent, the question is nonsensical. It isolates marriage more than it should. To truly understand the goal of marriage, it must be understood in the context of the human condition. There is a divine purpose for humanity. All marriages are relationships involving people. Marriage then must at its core contribute to that divine purpose.

Earlier, we presented the purpose of humanity according to the Westminster Shorter Catechism. "Man's chief end is to glorify God, and enjoy him forever." How then does one glorify God?

Well, what does glorify mean? According to dictionary.com glorify means:

1. To cause to be or treat as being more splendid, excellent, etc., than would normally be considered.

2. To honor with praise, admiration, or worship; extol.
3. To make glorious; invest with glory.[23]

With this definition it would be easy to assume that the chief end of man is to sing worship songs and say good things about God. That, however, is far too limited a view. Take a look at what the Apostle Paul said to the church in Corinth about this:

> For you were bought at a price. Therefore glorify God with your body. 1 Corinthians 6:20

> So whether you eat or drink, or whatever you do, do everything for the glory of God. 1 Corinthians 10:31

Paul clearly intended that glorifying God was a lifestyle not a recurring event. Glorifying God is something that should be consistent in your life, not just something that happens on Sunday mornings at a church building.

In the Ancient Near East, worship meant animal sacrifice. Different cultures had different ideas about what the animal sacrifice did, but all agreed that this was how you worshipped. This was true of the early Jews. In particular you can read Genesis and see all the times people worshipped God through sacrifice. God, however, expanded the definition of worship:

> The sacrifices God desires are a humble spirit
> O God, a humble and repentant heart you will not reject.
> Psalm 51:17

> What can we bring to the Lord?
> Should we bring him burnt offerings?
> Should we bow before God Most High
> with offerings of yearling calves?
> Should we offer him thousands of rams
> and ten thousand rivers of olive oil?
> Should we sacrifice our firstborn children
> to pay for our sins?

---

[23] https://www.dictionary.com/browse/glorify accessed Dec. 5, 2018

No, O people, the Lord has told you what is good,
and this is what he requires of you:
to do what is right, to love mercy,
and to walk humbly with your God. Micah 6:6-8 NLT

This can all be summed up simply in this phrase spoken by God to his people, "Be holy because I am holy" (Leviticus 11:44,45; 19:2; 20:7, 26; 21:8; Deuteronomy 23:14).

We glorify God by being holy. The goal of humanity is to become holy. The goal of marriage is to help you be the person you were created to be. The goal of marriage is to make you holy.

The Hebrew word for holy is קָדוֹשׁ (qadosh). You may have heard in a sermon that qadosh means to be separate or cut away from the whole. Holy people would, therefore, be separate from other people. There is some evidence for that but there is greater evidence for a different definition of qadosh. Qadosh is better defined as being clean, pure, or consecrated.[24] The way qadosh is used in the Bible, the best definition would be suitable to be used for or by God.

Holy people are suitable to be used by God. The goal of marriage is to make us more suitable to be used by God to fulfill his mission: the redemption of all things.

The Apostle Peter tells us what we need to be holy:

> Therefore, preparing your minds for action, and being sober-minded, set your hope fully on the grace that will be brought to you at the revelation of Jesus Christ. As obedient children, do not be conformed to the passions of your former ignorance, but as he who called you is holy, you also be holy in all your conduct, since it is written, «You shall be holy, for I am holy.» 1 Peter 1:13-16 ESV

To be holy, your minds need to be prepared to serve God in whatever capacity necessary. Your thoughts need to be clear, not clouded with things that are incompatible with the gospel. Your hope must be in the revelation of Jesus Christ, the one who died and rose again out of his great love for

---

[24] Theological Wordbook of the Old Testament

us and obedience to the Father. You must be obedient to God. You must avoid sin, particularly those temptations that so easily ensnared you before you were redeemed.

Preparing Your Minds for Action

Both thoughts of sin and thoughts of holiness start in our minds. Every word we say and every action we take starts with a thought in our minds. "Do not be conformed to this present world, but be transformed by the renewing of your mind, so that you may test and approve what is the will of God – what is good and well-pleasing and perfect" (Romans 12:2). For a person to be holy, their mind must be holy. Their mind must be suitable for God's work. This means Christians must discipline their thoughts to think godly thoughts and avoid ungodly ones. "We take every thought captive to make it obey Christ" (2 Corinthians 10:5b).

Of course, a good first step to renewing your mind and taking every thought captive is reading Scripture. Immersing yourself in God's word is the primary way to discipline your mind. The more you read God's thoughts, the more you will think about God's thoughts. The more you think about God's thoughts, the more you will think godly thoughts.

Your spouse, however, is another great resource God has given you to discipline your mind. There is no one you can trust more with your deepest thoughts than the person you married. No one will be as honest about your successes and failures either. But here's the catch: you have to be open with your spouse. You have to share your thoughts with your spouse, the good as well as the bad. You have to let them see what is going on underneath and give them permission to lovingly evaluate and correct so that your mind will be prepared for action.

You must also be the kind of person with whom it is safe for your spouse to share their deepest and darkest thoughts. You must develop the skill to listen nonjudgmentally and lovingly evaluate and sometimes correct. This is not an easy thing to do. No one likes to be corrected. Everyone is afraid of being vulnerable. You build your credibility as a safe person in every interaction you have together. The way you talk about each other to your friends and coworkers affects your ability to help each other become more holy. The way you love each other in every moment: the good times, the tough times, the times you feel so in love you might burst, the times you're so angry you want to scream. Every moment increases or decreases your strength as a couple to become more holy together. Every choice either helps or hurts your marriage's ability to thrive.

It is your choice. But the intent of marriage is to make you more holy. If you're going to follow God's intent, the choice is obvious.

Being Sober Minded

The second phrase in Peter's statement seems a little odd, "preparing your minds for action, and being sober-minded" (1 Peter 1:13a). If your mind is prepared to act, isn't it sober? Well, not necessarily. How many times have you acted without thinking? How many times have you regretted your actions because your judgment was clouded by emotion? It's hard to be holy when you are acting on instinct because your flesh, your sinful nature, is the part of you that leads you away from holiness. Often, the times you act on a strong emotion alone are the times you sin.

I (Bryon) find this particularly true when it comes to parenting. Our children are great, well-behaved, responsible children. But like all children, they make mistakes. One of the mistakes they make that is most likely to set me off is being disrespectful towards me or Jen. I will not tolerate disrespectful behavior. I know that sometimes they are upset or their feelings are hurt but that does not give them license to behave disrespectfully. At times, my emotions get in the way and I act rashly. My tone in correcting them can be too severe to be effective. Likewise, the consequences I implement can be too harsh to meet my desired goal. At those times, I am not sober minded. My capacity to think and behave in a godly manner is diminished because I have allowed my emotional state to cloud my judgment.

To make these "sober-minded" decisions, you must not only be prepared for action but your mind must also be clear of the things that would lead you to act in ungodly ways. This is another place where marriage helps you to be holy. Jen knows Bryon's tendencies. She knows the things that are likely to trigger an emotional response. After 17 years of marriage she also knows how to help him work through those issues. Sometimes the right response is to intervene immediately. Sometimes the right response is to discuss after the fact. In either case, she uses her relationship with him to help him process his emotions. She helps him along to become more holy.

The longer you are together and the closer you grow to each other, the more you will see temptations and sins that so easily entangle your partner. More than anyone else in the world, you have the opportunity to help them overcome their sinful nature. Through loving intervention, you can help them see their faults and grow into the person God created them to be.

This, of course, requires significant work by the Holy Spirit. You do not make your spouse holy. God makes them holy. You do not and cannot change your spouse. The Holy Spirit working in them changes them. You, however, have the ability to help them be open to what the Holy Spirit is doing in them through your words and actions.

The Holy Spirit must, therefore, also be working in you. You must be open to being changed by the Holy Spirit to become more holy yourself. Only as you are becoming the holy person God created you to be are you able to guide your spouse to be more holy. And your spouse, becoming the holy person God created them to be, can then help guide you to be more holy.

There is a mutuality in this. It is not up to one spouse to be the instigator to make the other holy. It is not your job to make your spouse holy. It is not your spouse's job to make you holy. You were by nature both fallen, sinful people in desperate need of God so that you could become who you were created to be. Through Christ, you have the power to overcome your sinful nature. Your identity is no longer sinner. Your identity is beloved child of God. Now, be holy as your Father is holy. Your marriage and your spouse are resources that God will use to make you both holy and develop in holiness for His glory. As you become more holy, you are able to lead your spouse towards holiness and your spouse will be able to lead you towards holiness. Together as you become more holy you will help each other grow in holiness. You create a cycle of growing holiness together.

Do Not Comply with Evil Urges

1 Corinthians 10:13 states, "No temptation has overtaken you that is not common to man" (ESV). This means that the temptations you face

are not completely unique to you. All people everywhere face temptation. Many people think that the temptation they face is unique to them. They think that no one has ever been tempted in that way. No one can ever understand their temptation. These thoughts are never true!

These thoughts lead people to see themselves as distinct from other humans in their sin in the most negative way possible, leading to guilt and shame. There are two ways most people tend to respond to these thoughts. Some become disgusted by their sin and weakness. They see themselves as filthy and evil. They, therefore, are afraid to share the truth about their struggles because they do not want others to see them the same way they see themselves. They are afraid to share the ugly parts of their lives because they are afraid of appearing ugly to other people.

A second group of people sees other people struggling with temptation and sin and believes that there is no one to help them deal with their own sin. They either see others as too weak or overwhelmed to help them, or they see themselves as superior to others not needing help because there is no help worth receiving. In either case they avoid being honest with their temptation. They avoid being honest about their sin.

Whether one hides their sin because they are afraid to be viewed as dirty or weak, or one hides their sin because they think they must handle it on their own, both are falling into a trap. Sin flourishes in darkness. God never intended for you to deal with sin on your own. Sin is too heavy to carry on your own. That's why Paul said to the church in Galatia:

> Brothers and sisters, if a person is discovered in some sin, you who are spiritual restore such a person in a spirit of gentleness. Pay close attention to yourselves, so that you are not tempted too. Carry one another's burdens, and in this way you will fulfill the law of Christ" (Galatians 6:1-2).

Ok, we've established that your sin is not unique to you and that all Christians are called to support each other when tempted by sin. Now let's get back to what Peter was saying in 1 Peter 1. "As obedient children, do not be conformed to the passions of your former ignorance." Your temptation is not unique to you but the context in which you are tempted is unique to you. Your background, the life you have lived to this point, the sins you have committed in the past, your pride, your fear, your lust, all make you susceptible to certain temptations. Everyone is not equally tempted by every sin. For some sexual temptation is particularly strong. Others are tempted by anger. There are those that are particularly tempted by money and wealth. Many find themselves tempted by prestige. There is a unique mix of temptations to which you are weak. This weakness often comes from your past. Peter calls these the passions of your former ignorance. The ESV translation translates this phrase as "the evil urges you used to follow." Either way, you are susceptible to sin and have created a pattern of sin in your life.

This pattern of sin can be overcome by God's provision of grace to you. The passage quoted from 1 Corinthians earlier finishes saying, "God is faithful, and he will not let you be tempted beyond your ability, but with the temptation he will also provide the way of escape, that you may be able to endure it" (10:13b ESV). One of the things God has provided you to help you escape temptation is your spouse. Your spouse knows you. Your spouse knows your weaknesses. Over the past years living together they have seen your weaknesses. They have seen you overcome by temptation. They have seen you overcome temptation and can support you in overcoming temptation again and again.

The unique perspective your spouse has on your temptation and sin makes them the perfect person to help you avoid those evil urges of your former ignorance. Like many men, Bryon has been tempted by lust. Jen knows that the female body can be particularly tempting to Bryon because of patterns he formed in his youth. Bryon intentionally avoids situations where he would see images of women in various states of undress that would be tempting. Jen knows this. When we watch T.V. together there are occasionally scenes that it would be better if Bryon did not watch them. When those scenes occur, Bryon either looks away and Jen gives him any information that is pertinent to the plot or we fast forward through those scenes. If there is a show that has too much such content but the plot interests us both, Jen has no problem not watching the show because she would rather be with Bryon than watch the show on her own but she wants to support his efforts to avoid temptation.

The same can be true for you. To be holy, it is important that you avoid those evil urges from your former ignorance. The purpose of marriage is to help both of you grow in holiness. Because you know each other intimately you have the ability to support and protect each other from temptation and sin.

Hope in the Grace of Jesus Christ

We intentionally skipped over a phrase because we wanted to close this section with it. "Set your hope fully on the grace that will be brought to you at the revelation of Jesus Christ" (1 Peter 1:13c). This phrase is drawn from the fundamentals of Peter's theology. We won't delve too deeply into it here, because this is a book about marriage not a commentary on 1 Peter. The important thing to understand here is that Peter's faith is forward looking. The events of the past, specifically of Jesus' life, death, and resurrection, happened to facilitate a promise for the future. Peter is looking forward to the day when Jesus returns and all things are made new.

One day Jesus is going to return. Christians put their hope in a promise of a better future when Jesus returns and all things are made new. In that future, sin and death are destroyed. Relationships between people and God and between God's people themselves will be restored. The sin that impedes relationships from being all that they should be will be gone. The sin that causes strife in marriages will be gone. There is no way for anyone to know what relationships will be like when Jesus returns. We know that relationships will be free of evil and sin. We put our hope in that promise.

There are times when the challenge to grow in holiness will be overwhelming. Some days it is hard to be open and vulnerable with your spouse. Some days it's even harder to be loving and encouraging when your spouse is struggling and you need to support them. There will be days when you are tempted to give up on the whole enterprise because growing in holiness together seems to be too much effort. In those days, place your hope in the grace that will be revealed in Jesus. The work to become more holy will be fulfilled in the day when we are living in the kingdom that we are preparing to live in today. We are becoming suitable to be citizens in God's new kingdom that he will bring about when Jesus returns.

Conclusion

Marriage is an amazing gift from God. Having a person with whom to share your life is one of the greatest blessings available to you. God wants you to enjoy your marriage and be happy together for the rest of your lives. God's goal for your marriage, however, is not for you to be happy.

Happiness is a horrible goal. It is impossible to control. It is fleeting and will never be maintained perpetually. If the goal of marriage is happiness then every marriage has failed.

Happiness is not the goal of marriage. Holiness is the goal of marriage. Holiness is the goal of this life. Your purpose in this life is to continue to become more suitable for the work and kingdom of God. But can we share this amazing truth with you as well? As we become more of what God created us to be in holiness, we enter into a sustained state of joy, peace, and love that transcends a fleeting happiness. Indeed, holiness is far better than happiness!

Marriage is a unique relationship that can help you become more holy. There is no one in your life who has greater access to the truth about your life. Also, no one has the potential to influence you in the way your spouse can. Because of the intimate nature of a marriage your spouse has great potential to help you become more holy. Likewise, you have huge potential to help your spouse become more holy as well.

Action step:

Our challenge to you is to discuss together how you will be more purposeful in growing more holy together.

CHAPTER 5

BECOMING ONE

The first section of this book has been very theological. We had to describe the context in which *Operation: Thriving Marriage* would be executed. It was important to lay the theological foundation of marriage before we get into the more practical section of the book. We have found in life that people are more likely to follow through on the "how" if they have a good "what" and "why." We think you will be more likely to take action based on the information provided in the following chapters if you have a firm grasp on the purpose of marriage outlined in the previous chapters.

Now that we've described where *Operation: Thriving Marriage* will take place, now we will describe the tactics that will make it successful. We just discussed the theological aspect of becoming one in the previous chapters. In one sense, oneness occurs when you're married. In chapter 2, we talked about the new spiritual reality of life once you're married. Oneness is not only an event; it is also a journey. The rest of this book will help you become one together. It will provide you with skills and resources to help you on the life-long journey towards oneness.

Return on Investment

Jen worked on a really rough divorce case several years ago where she represented the husband. Both the husband and wife were about the same height and build. They were both rather scrappy and always ready for a fight, and Jen deduced that they both likely beat each other up after together consuming way too much alcohol. During their marriage, they verbally sparred over how the other spent money. Each withdrew large amounts of cash from their joint accounts, and complained to their respective lawyers about how selfish the other one was while simultaneously buying things that would never benefit the other. It's no surprise that their marriage eventually fell apart.

We all have needs that can only be met by the resources in the marriage. In the "me against you" approach of the couple above each person fights to ensure their needs and desires are met by the resources in the marriage. The cost to the other person is the price of being in the marriage. Ultimately, everyone pays a price to be in the marriage and the hope is that the price never becomes so high that the cost of marriage outweighs the value of the marriage. In this case everyone is constantly evaluating their return on investment (ROI).

Constantly evaluating the ROI of your marriage is a recipe for disaster and divorce. When two people focus on pulling what they need and want out of the marriage and their spouse, it creates both a sense of entitlement and a sense of disdain. Feelings of entitlement develop because you feel you deserve to get everything you want and feelings of disdain because your partner is never able to give you everything you want. Ultimately, it leaves both people depleted, lacking, and wanting, much like a vehicle with an empty gas tank.

To have the marriage that you want and that God intends for you, you have to break out of the ROI perspective that most people have about marriage and virtually every other relationship. A healthy marriage cannot exist in a "me vs. you" environment. The only way to have a healthy marriage is to see yourselves together as a team in every aspect of your marriage.

This first hit home with us on our wedding day. Our wedding was officiated by Jen's mentor and a dear friend of ours. During the ceremony, he shared some words of encouragement with us. He observed that during the several years he had known us we were each other's biggest cheerleaders. We had always been a good team. At the time, we didn't know how important those words would be to us.

With those few words, our friend gave us an identity as a couple that has influenced us throughout our marriage. We are a team. In everything we do, we focus on how it affects us as a team. Neither of us makes a decision without considering the other and significant decisions are always made together.

Developing Your Team

A team is actually a very good metaphor for the oneness that is marriage. Think of your favorite team. Bryon's is the Detroit Red Wings. Jen's is Chip and Joanna from HGTV's *Fixer Upper*. A good team functions as one unit. It is made up of two or more unique individuals but they together function as one. They, moreover, accomplish things together that none of them could do alone.

Functioning as one is, however, a process. It is not something that happens overnight. You've been on teams before, work teams, sports teams, volunteer teams. Everyone has been on some sort of team. All teams develop. No team functions at peak capacity immediately. It takes time for the team to become what they can and will be.

You may have heard at some point about the stages of team development. It's a theory developed by Bruce Tuckman in the 1960s.[25] He argues that every team goes through five stages of development. The first stage is forming. In this stage no one really knows each other and they don't know where they fit in. There is very little trust at this stage and everyone is putting their best foot forward. Everyone is trying to figure out where they fit in the team.

This is the "honeymoon" stage. The team members at this stage are trying to impress each other. No one wants to assert themselves because everyone is trying to be liked. Many teams falsely think that the team dynamic is great because there is no conflict. That thought on teams and in marriage is completely false. If there is no conflict, then there is no honest communication. It doesn't matter how long you've known each other or how much you love each other, there is no relationship where

---

[25] M. K. Smith, Bruce W. Tuckman – <u>Forming, Storming, Norming and Performing in Groups</u>, *Infed.org: Education, Community-Building and Change*, (<u>https://infed.org/mobi/bruce-w-tuckman-forming-storming-norming-and-performing-in-groups/</u>) accessed May 26, 2020.

everyone is 100% in sync all the time. Often couples will try to artificially extend this stage because they fear conflict. Ultimately that leads to deeper issues later on in the relationship as concerns and dissatisfaction are not addressed and fester. Ultimately, when dissatisfaction builds up there will be a problem. If dissatisfaction builds up for too long it is very difficult to overcome because the dissatisfied individual loses faith that it is possible to overcome the issues.

It's tempting to think that this forming phase is completed during the dating phase of the relationship. That, unfortunately, is inaccurate. As we stated in earlier chapters, your relationship changed significantly when you got married. Those changes move your relationship back into the forming stage. While there may not be outward signs of a lack of trust, both individuals are still putting their best foot forward and trying to figure out what their role is in the marriage.

This is why we are such strong proponents of the right kind of premarital counseling. Our goal in premarital counseling isn't to provide answers to specific questions but rather create the environment where a couple learns how to navigate issues together. Premarital counseling is not a process to resolve issues in a relationship. It is a process teaching the couple how to work through issues together.

The second phase in team development is storming. In the storming phase, team members are confident of their competency and are in process of determining what their role is on the team. At this point individuals are claiming turf and asserting authority. Trust is still rather low. The thought that most people on the team have is that if they don't do it, tasks won't get done. The more dominant people will try to actively control how the team functions. People with less dominant preferences will try to control situations passive-aggressively. A lot of arguments happen during this stage. The arguments tend to be unproductive because they are often more personal rather than objective focused.

It is often said that the first year of marriage is the most difficult. That is usually because the couple is going through the storming phase of their relationship. Some couples despair at this point because what seemed so simple and natural in the beginning is becoming hard. Feelings of romance and satisfaction fade as conflict increases.

The most important thing to remember about this is that it is normal and healthy. Of course, "claiming turf and asserting authority" is not what should be done in a marriage. Couples should work together to define roles and responsibilities in an open and compassionate way. No one should be looking to control the relationship or act passive-aggressively, either. Instead, couples should be working together to maximize their strengths. Unfortunately, storming exists in marriages but keep in mind that it can be handled kindly, respectfully, and calmly in its best days. Remember, it is not normal or healthy to agree on everything all the time. The fact that there is conflict is evidence of honesty. Successfully navigating the storming phase in your relationship will make your marriage stronger. This phase will teach you that you can overcome disagreements. It will also help you develop the communication and conflict resolution skills that you will need to have a healthy marriage that will last a lifetime.

The problems come in at this stage when couples have not learned how to communicate in healthy ways. Unhealthy communication increases conflict because now the couple is arguing over two issues. The first issue is the <u>original cause</u> of the disagreement, <u>Problem A</u>. The second is the <u>poor communication techniques</u> that have surfaced during the conflict, <u>Problem B</u>.

Most conflicts that create marital problems deal with Problem B conflicts. Problem A conflicts are often easy to resolve. They usually involve compromise or clarification about a task of function. They deal with what you're going to do. Problem Bs are a lot harder. They involve how you treat each other. The Problem B problems are the ones that lead you to feel unloved or disrespected. They are the ones that need to be dealt with most for your marriage to be healthy. We will come back to this concept in a later chapter.

Storming is normal and healthy for a time. This phase is prolonged by a lack of communication and conflict resolution skills. We believe all marriages can get past this stage with a refocus on the relationship and good communication and conflict resolution skills. We will talk more about those later in this book.

Sadly, we have seen marriages end because they never get past this storming stage. They remember the excitement and romance that happened earlier in the relationship and fear it will never return. If you're in the storming phase now and feel like it will never end, keep reading. Together you can get through this and your marriage will be stronger and healthier because you did.

The third phase is norming. Norming happens when teams healthily pass through the storming phase. The result of the conflict, turf wars, and shows of dominance is that team members know where they fit relationally and what roles they need to fill on the team. Team members now know the skills and competencies everyone brings to the team. A healthy division of labor is created. Trust begins to build as the team starts functioning more efficiently and tasks are being accomplished. There is, however, some apprehension. The memories of storming are still fresh. Team members may fear going back into the storming phase and are careful to avoid triggering arguments. Communication is more open than in the forming phase but can still be tentative.

At this point in marriage, life at home is normalized. The division of labor for chores is clear. Routine has started to set in. If you successfully navigated the storming phase, disagreements are less explosive and focus more on Problem As than Problem Bs. Problem Bs still crop up but are handled more quickly and easily with less strife.

Communication in the marriage during this time can still be tentative. It's natural to want to avoid topics at this point because you want to avoid the argument. It just doesn't seem worth it. Don't fall into that trap. Just because you have successfully navigated the storming phase doesn't mean you can't move backwards. It is always possible to go back to an earlier phase in the relationship based on a new context. Unresolved issues will easily take you right back to forming or storming.

The next phase is the most comfortable phase. Tuckman called it the performing phase. At this point the team is firing on all cylinders. Everything is functioning well. Tasks are getting done efficiently. There is a high level of creativity and synergy on the team. Communication is open and free.

This is a very fulfilling time in marriage. As a couple you feel closer to each other than at any other time. Because you feel supremely safe with each other there are still disagreements, even arguments, but in the end they are completely resolved. When an argument is over, it's over. There are no issues lingering. Together you are content and at peace enjoying the life together that God has given you.

Sound too good to be true? It's not. We have seen many couples experience this stage in their marriage and have found ourselves in this stage as well. This is what marriage looks like when everything is working as God intended. This is what marriage looks like when it is thriving. It's not a pipe dream. It is real. We believe if you apply what you are learning in this book you will experience this stage more and more frequently.

Stage five in Tuckman's model is adjourning. The purpose for which the team assembled is over. It may be because the purpose was timebond and the time has ended or because the tasks have all been completed. The team may be broken up because team members leave to join new teams or their roles in the organization change. Clearly, this "adjourning" stage doesn't apply to marriage. This isn't a free pass to get divorced; sorry, not sorry.

We prefer to call the fifth stage in marriage reforming. One thing we can guarantee about your marriage is that it is going to change. The context in which you operate as a couple will change. One of you may change jobs. You may move to a new city, or just another home in your current city. You may have children. Your parents will die one day. Things in your life are going to change. These changes are going to affect your relationship.

Some changes will not be too dramatic. You will navigate through them quickly discussing the situation and implications without missing a step. You will meet the new challenges and move through without noticing. It will feel like you never left the performing stage. In actuality, the skills you developed in the other stages and the limited scope of the change allowed you to navigate the reforming stage quickly and easily without any issues.

Other changes will be more significant. They will have a greater impact on your lives. These changes will bump you back to an earlier phase in your relationship. You will repeat in a new context many of the same experiences you had before. Hopefully you learned the lessons you needed when you were in the stage before and navigate it more easily this time.

It is very important to note that returning to an earlier phase in Tuckman's model says nothing about the health of your marriage. The healthiest marriages need to go back through the forming, storming, and norming phases when they experience significant life changes. That's the only way to appropriately and practically navigate these changes.

Having a child is the most obvious example. Even in the healthiest marriage a new child changes the relationship significantly and almost every couple will go back to the forming stage. Parents are learning what it means to be mom and dad. Spouses are learning what it means to be the husband/wife to a new mom/dad. There are new tasks and chores that must be accomplished. Together couples have to figure out how to do all of this and it is never completely the way they imagined it would be.

Through all the changes and challenges of marriage, if you look at it as a process of becoming one, you will learn the skills you need to accomplish your goal. As you work together as a team, you will have a thriving marriage that will last a lifetime.

Conclusion

Let's go back to the idea of oneness. Becoming one is a process. Throughout your marriage oneness will ebb and flow. A marriage isn't a math problem. There isn't one right answer to an equation of $1 + 1 = 1$.

There is, however, a typical process for married couples who grow into their marriage. This process is similar to Tuckman's Stages of Group Development. When you successfully navigate these phases you grow closer in oneness. Your oneness is not static but will constantly change and yes, this is healthy as life circumstances change. In this life you will never be completely one at all times. Instead, you will be more or less one at different times throughout your lives together. The rest of this book will give you tools and skills to navigate these phases in your relationship and develop this oneness in your marriage.

Action step:

- Discuss together what stage of marriage you are in right now.
- What steps can you take to best support each other?
- How can you move to the next stage in a healthy way?
- If you are in the performing stage, what events do you see in the future that may take you to the reforming stage

CHAPTER 6

TEAM MARRIAGE

In the late 2000s and early 2010s the *Twilight* movies were a major cultural phenomenon. If you're not familiar with the series, it's an angsty teen drama that centers around a teenage girl and her feelings towards a vampire and a werewolf. So will she end up with the vampire or the werewolf?

During the height of the movies' popularity, two factions of fans formed. One faction wanted the girl, Bella, to choose the vampire, Edward. The other wanted Bella to choose the werewolf, Jacob. The groups were referred to as Team Edward and Team Jacob. Merchandisers, of course, loved the phenomenon. Team Edward and Team Jacob merchandise was everywhere. Once you chose a character to root for as her love interest, that was your team. You were committed to seeing Bella fall in love with and be with that character.

While creating opposing teams and pitting them against each other is a great marketing strategy and sells a lot of merchandise, it's a horrible model for a marriage. Team Husband versus Team Wife doesn't fare well for the marriage relationship. Rarely do we hear people communicating about their marriage in such stark adversarial terms unless they are meeting with Jen about representation in a divorce case.

We have, however, seen couples display this kind of behavior all over the place. While couples may never say their marriage is adversarial, many act as if it was. They make demands staking out their turf in the marriage. They use money, children, or sex as tools to manipulate each other to get what they want. They are constantly bargaining or negotiating for #1 alone. They approach their marriage from a scarcity mindset seeking to ensure they come out ahead in the marriage. Marriages like this usually end in divorce, but even when they don't the people involved never experience the fullness of marriage that God has made available to them.

The marriages we just described are a lot like the fans of the *Twilight* movies. They unintentionally create a me vs. you environment. Team husband vs. team wife. If this continues and children are born the parents start competing for additional team members which puts the children in the horrible place of having to choose between team mom and team dad. The way to overcome this experience or completely prevent it if it hasn't formed in your marriage is to abandon the Team Husband/Team Wife, me vs. you mindset and instead develop a new mindset: a Team Marriage mindset.

Our philosophy of Team Marriage is at the core of what we believe is necessary to experience the healthy marriage that God intends for you. It's the primary tool we use to trap that pesky second fox. In a nutshell, a Team Marriage mindset requires that both husband and wife place their marriage and their relationship above their own personal desires. This isn't just some gimmick that we've come up with to sell books either. It's actually central to being Christian and having a Christian marriage.

Biblical Foundation of Team Marriage

The root of Christianity is selflessness. It starts with Jesus and what he did to redeem our fallen humanity. Christ is our perfect example of selflessness. He demonstrated selflessness by taking on flesh, living amongst us, and giving up his life as a ransom for us.The beginning of the Gospel of John lays it out beautifully. At the beginning of creation, Jesus was there creating all that is.

> In the beginning was the Word, and the Word was with God, and the Word was fully God. The Word was with God in the beginning. All things were created by him, and apart from him not one thing was created that has been created. John 1:1-3

Before his incarnation, Jesus existed in perfect love and harmony in the presence of God the Father and the Holy Spirit. Out of love for the brothers and sisters he created, he sacrificed his peace and comfort to live among those he created.

> Now the Word became flesh and took up residence among us. We saw his glory – the glory of the one and only, full of grace and truth, who came from the Father. John 1:14

> [Jesus] though he existed in the form of God
> did not regard equality with God
> as something to be grasped,
> but emptied himself
> by taking on the form of a slave,
> and by sharing in human nature. Philippians 2:6-7

Jesus' purpose in becoming human was simple. He came to serve and to die for the sake of humanity.

> For even the Son of Man did not come to be served but to serve, and to give his life as a ransom for many. Mark 10:45

> He humbled himself,
> by becoming obedient to the point of death
> – even death on a cross! Phillipians 2:8

To be a Christian doesn't mean to merely acknowledge Jesus as God. Being Christian means to follow Jesus and to be like Jesus. A Christian is one that lives their life in response to and in imitation of the life of Jesus. Jesus said it himself, "I give you a new commandment – to love one another. Just as I have loved you, you also are to love one another. Everyone will know by this that you are my disciples – if you have love for one another" (John 13:34-35).

To be a Christian means to love others like Jesus loves them. It means to love self-sacrificially. It means to put others' needs before your own.

Instead of being motivated by selfish ambition or vanity, each of you should, in humility, be moved to treat one another as more important than yourself. Each of you should be concerned not only about your own interests, but about the interests of others as well. You should have the same attitude toward one another that Christ Jesus had. Philippians 2:3-4

By definition Christians love sacrificially. Christian marriage, therefore, is a marriage in which the husband and wife love each other sacrificially.

Developing a Team Marriage Mindset

This Team Marriage thing sounds good, but how does it work practically? How do we develop Team Marriage? It starts with developing a Team Marriage mindset. The thoughts we think are fundamental to the actions we take. It's so fundamental that the elementary school our children attend has restructured their educational model to teach children how to have a growth mindset. A growth mindset teaches children to think that they have the ability to learn and improve rather than a closed mindset thinking they have a limited intellect and can only learn so much then are unable to improve. Children with a growth mindset are more successful in school because they believe they can be successful. Our mindset has everything to do with our actions. Our actions follow our mindset.

This reflects what the Apostle Paul said about spiritual formation in Romans, "Do not be conformed to this present world, but be transformed by the renewing of your mind, so that you may test and approve what is the will of God—what is good and well-pleasing and perfect" (12:2). Our thoughts determine our actions. What are your thoughts about marriage? What are your actions that follow?

Presuming Good Will

With that in mind, the first thing we tell couples to do to develop a Team Marriage mindset is to develop a presupposition of good will. Here's what we mean. Many couples talk about all of the things their spouse does that bother them. They focus on the little actions that are annoying. They focus on the actions that end up having negative outcomes.

For instance, often one spouse is responsible for the laundry. If you believe the detergent commercials, it's the wife, but we know that isn't always the case. Anyway, certain garments have special handling considerations. Perhaps they are dry clean only. Maybe they have to air dry. Perhaps there's a stain on a shirt. When the spouse that doesn't normally do the laundry does the laundry, they may not follow the special handling considerations. When this happens, the garment is often ruined. Invariably, the ruined garment is a favorite in the wardrobe.

Well, that's fantastic! Grrrrrrr! Your favorite shirt was just ruined! It didn't *have* to be ruined. If they had just paid attention to the tag, or looked for stains before starting the laundry you wouldn't be in this situation anymore. They are so careless and inconsiderate! How could they have been so foolish?!

That is not a Team Marriage mindset. That is not a presupposition of good will. It presumes a disregard of what is important to you. Those types of thoughts are bound to create feelings of bitterness and likely to cause an argument. If left unaddressed, they can destroy a marriage.

A presupposition of good will presumes that the offending spouse was trying to be helpful. Rather than looking at the mistake, it presumes a positive intent behind the action. The person doing laundry was trying to be helpful. They were trying to express love. They wanted things to go well.

When you presume good will, you think that the actions taken and the words said are coming from a place of love and care. You presume that your partner is not trying to be hurtful, spiteful, or mean. You presume that they love you and want a positive marriage. They are just not communicating it in the right way.

When you approach your spouse with a presupposition of good will, you look for the positive aspects in the things they say and do. The more you look for positive loving aspects in your spouse the more you will see loving things in them. The more you see love coming from them the more you will feel loved by them. The more you feel loved the more loving you will be towards them.

This does not mean that you ignore things that bother you. It does not mean you fail to address actions that have negative consequences. It is important to deal with those things and we will discuss that more in a later chapter. At this point the important thing to remember is, your spouse is not trying to ruin your life, or your marriage. They love you and want to have a healthy lifelong marriage with you.

It's like being on any team. When the team presumes everyone is working towards the same goal, they are willing to forgive actions that detract from the goal because they know their teammate wants the same thing they do. Their teammate merely made a mistake this time around and there is room for improvement the next time.

Focusing on Each Other's Needs

The second way to develop a Team Marriage mindset is to focus on the needs of your spouse over your own personal needs. This goes directly back to Philippians 2:4, "Each of you should be concerned not only about your own interests, but about the interests of others as well."

Imagine for a moment two people each carrying a bag. In this bag they carry all the resources they have to meet the marital needs of their spouse. The focus of both is to find ways to get what they need out of the other's bag. They use any strategy they can think of to get things out of the bag. They ask. They take. They lie. They manipulate. Eventually both bags will be empty. Yet, each person will still be reaching into the other's bag and finding it empty. They will be disappointed that their needs aren't met and frustrated that their spouse isn't meeting their needs.

That's a miserable way to live. There is, however, another way. Imagine the same two people carrying the same two bags. This time, instead of finding ways to take things from the other bag, both individuals focus on filling the other's bag. In this situation, there is no increase in the amount of resources available but no bag is ever empty because together the couple is constantly putting things in the other's bag. They are so focused on meeting each other's needs that both individual's needs are always met. That's a Team Marriage mindset!

Having a Team Marriage mindset means focusing on your spouse's needs over your own needs. Yes, this is a very unnatural way to view things. We are conditioned by our culture that we need to look out for ourselves and let everyone else look out for themselves. But looking out for the needs of others is the countercultural upside down way of life that Jesus intends for us to live. This is the kind of marriage Jesus intends for us to have.

It's important for us to note that no human being can meet all of your needs. Only God can do that! If you rely on any person, including your spouse, to meet all your needs, you will be sadly disappointed. Still, in the marriage relationship, there are emotional and relational needs that can and should be met by your spouse and you should meet these needs for your spouse as well. That's why this takes Team Marriage effort for mutual edification for each of you and in turn for your marriage.

To live out Team Marriage this way requires both great trust and great focus. You have to trust that your spouse is doing everything they can to meet your needs. In those days when your needs aren't met, it's not because they're not trying to meet them. It's because they simply don't know how or may not even know those needs exist. You also have to focus. You have to focus on your spouse. You have to focus on learning what their needs are and focus on meeting them. Often this conversation narrows to be a conversation about sex, but there are other relational needs that you and your partner have. In fact, when those other needs are being met, the sexual needs often are also met. Every person is unique and they will express their needs in different ways. You need to watch, listen, ask questions, and learn your spouse's needs, how they communicate them, and how to meet them. Be vocal about your needs as well. You need to be open about your needs so your spouse is able to meet them.

Bryon is an introvert and can get overwhelmed by large gatherings and parties. Jen as an extrovert can make the rounds but can also either quickly tire or get involved in some great conversations and not want to leave so quickly. We've come up with codes to signal each other that it's time to leave the event, with the one who wants to leave being given a margin of time to wrap up the conversations. We won't tell you what the signal is, though, for concern you'd see us use it at some point. Suffice it to say: whether it's leaving a party, getting time to talk with your spouse about concerns, having scheduled family time, dealing with money management issues or in-laws, make sure that you vocalize your needs and that you create a safe relationship for your spouse to discuss their needs as well.

Then address them together and come to the best resolution for both of you as a couple.

Conclusion

Couples often approach their relationship in a me vs. you mindset. Although they would never express it so starkly their actions show it to be true. They are focused on getting what they want and need out of the relationship. Their focus is on themselves because that is how they have been taught to live.

Me vs. you is not the way Jesus taught us to live in any relationship, especially not marriage! Jesus instead taught us to live self-sacrificially; considering others better than ourselves. We summarize this idea in marriage with the concept of Team Marriage. A Team Marriage mindset always presumes goodwill in the other and focuses on meeting the other's needs rather than getting them to meet yours. If you both act as such, both spouses' needs will be met and you will be able to act as a more dynamic partnership with abundant resources from each of you.

Action step:

- Discuss with your spouse your unmet needs and in turn, what your spouse's unmet needs in your marriage are.
- How can each of you help to meet these needs?

CHAPTER 7

BEING YOU WHEN YOU'RE US

One of the most fascinating and confusing things about the Christian belief in God is the trinity. It's a mystery how one God can eternally exist as three unique persons. Christians not only believe that each person in the trinity has a unique role but that they are unique individuals. Each individual in the trinity has all of the aspects of personhood. They each have their own identity, role, and relationship to the other members of the trinity and creation.

In chapter one, we talked about how in marriage we experience something of the eternal relationship of the trinity. In marriage, two individuals become one couple. The two have a new identity. Everything that each individual thinks and does must now be processed in the context of them as a couple.

Yet, the couple does not cease to be individuals. The identity of the individuals is not annihilated. It is expanded. The goals, dreams, and passions of each individual in the couple are not eliminated. They are placed into a greater context.

As a couple you need to be a team. Being a team does not, however, eliminate the uniqueness and differences of each person. It rather embraces, values, and enhances those differences in a way that empowers and uplifts them to help the individuals become fully the people they were created to be.

Being Us Does Not Mean You Stop Being You

Let's go back to the beginning again and look at the creation of humanity. When God created us, he created each individual to be unique and special.

> Then God said, "Let us make humankind in our image, after our likeness, so they may rule over the fish of the sea and the birds of the air, over the cattle, and over all the earth, and over all the creatures that move on the earth."
>
> God created humankind in his own image,
> in the image of God he created them,
> *male and female he created them.*
>
> God blessed them and said to them, "Be fruitful and multiply! Fill the earth and subdue it! Rule over the fish of the sea and the birds of the air and every creature that moves on the ground." (Genesis 1:26-28, *emphasis added*).

From the beginning, God created humans with differences. Then he blessed them and gave them their purpose. Their purpose was to fill the earth and subdue it. Their purpose was not to become the same. Rather their purpose was to bring and maintain order in God's creation as his image-bearers. This required that they exercise their uniqueness for the furtherance of God's vision. Just as God has eternally existed as three unique persons accomplishing his plan, humans are to live in marriage as unique persons accomplishing God's plans.

Becoming one does not mean losing yourself in your new identity as a couple. Healthy relationships embrace and encourage differences. Oneness is not sameness, but rather lovingly embracing each other's differences for the glory of God.

It is not healthy for an individual to completely lose their identity in their relationship. We have seen this happen in marriages, in dating, and even in friendships. You may have seen this at some point too. Those relationships are clearly unhealthy.

When a person completely loses their identity in a relationship, one of two things is usually happening. First, we have seen one person in the relationship be so dominant that the other person's identity is fully found in their relationship to the dominant person. The dominant individual insists on the other submitting fully. This is an abusive relationship. Abuse is not just physical. Abuse can take on many forms and can happen in any relationship. If an individual demands full submission or dismisses the other's wants and needs as less important or not important at all, this is not a healthy relationship and could be an abusive relationship.

The second way we have seen individuals completely consumed by their identity as their relationship is when they place their personal value completely in the hands of another person. In this case they have little to no self-esteem. They get their entire worth from another person. They are voluntarily submissive because their identity is found in being needed by another. This is called codependence. One person depends on being needed by another and cannot see themselves as anything other than in relationship to and needed by another.[26]

Clearly, neither of these unhealthy relationships are what God intends for you. Rather, God intends for marriage to be a place where your unique identity in Christ is more fully experienced and expressed.

All of us are unique individuals created by God to be exactly who we are. When you got married you became a couple but didn't stop being individuals. As you grow closer and embrace your identity as a couple, never lose your identity as an individual. Keeping your individual identity is vital to being a healthy couple.

Embracing Differences

It is important that you do not allow your uniqueness to be overwhelmed by your identity as a couple. It is equally important that you embrace the differences in your partner. These are two sides of the same coin but the actions are very different. In the section above we talked about not

---

[26] If you are reading this book and find yourself in either of these scenarios, please take the time to talk to someone who can help you. We highly recommend discussing this with a Christian therapist or counselor who can give you an objective perspective on your relationship and tools to help you.

allowing yourself to be overcome by your new identity as a couple. In this section we will talk about encouraging the differences in your spouse.

It is tempting to fight against the differences between two partners in a marriage. Things would be simpler *if he would do things my way*. We would fight less *if she didn't respond that way*. I wish he was more like me. I wish she felt the way I do.

The reality is, none of that is true. To a great extent, the reason you are attracted to each other is found in the differences between you. The things that surprise, comfort, and excite you are often the things you see in your partner that are not naturally part of you. "It's not the differences between partners that cause problems but how the differences are handled when they arise."[27]

While you may think that the differences between you cause problems in your relationship, it is not truly the differences between you. It is instead the way you interact together regarding those differences. When Bryon was a student in the United States Air Force Senior Non-Commissioned Officer Academy (AFSNCOA) they discussed this as Problem A and Problem B. We introduced this idea in chapter 5. We're coming back to it here because it's an important concept to accomplish Mission Two: Becoming One.

<u>Problem A</u> is the problem you are <u>trying to solve</u>. A couple years ago we were trying to decide how to deal with an issue our son faced at school. Our son and his friends collect Pokemon Cards. Part of the experience is trading cards with each other. Unfortunately, when you're in second grade, it is easy to experience buyers remorse over a trade. The emotions tied to this can be rather intense. The question regarding how we should handle our son trading Pokemon Cards at school is problem A.

<u>Problem B</u> is the problem <u>that develops between two people who have different perspectives</u> on Problem A. In the case above Problem B developed because the two of us had different views about the value of Pokemon Cards and with how they should be played.

Jen did not like the idea of trading Pokemon Cards at all. We bought

---

27 Clifford Notarius and Howard J. Markman, *We Can Work It Out* (New York: Perigree, 1993), 22, qtd in Jaes L. Furrow, and Cameron Lee, *Preparing Couples for Love and Marriage: A Pastor's Resource*, (Nashville, TN: Abingdon Press, 2013), 36) Kindle Edition.

specific sets for our son so he could get specific cards. Those cards had greater perceived value than other cards. It was hard, however, to determine the actual value of a given card. Our son could, therefore, potentially be taken advantage of by trading a valuable card for a less valuable one. Moreover, we bought the cards for our son's enjoyment and trading was unnecessary.

Bryon felt differently. Bryon had fond memories of trading different collectible cards when he was a young boy. To him, the full experience of enjoying Pokemon Cards was trading them.

Therein lay problem B. Problem A was should our son trade Pokemon Cards. Problem B was our different views on the purpose of Pokemon Cards and the value of trading. We had many conversations discussing our perspectives. Everytime the conversation revolved around Problem B. We did not agree on whether trading was or was not an integral aspect of playing with Pokemon cards. Ultimately, we decided not to let him trade because of the disruption it was creating in the friend group when one of the boys had buyers remorse after a trade.

Here is the point of all of this: the most difficult arguments you will face in your marriage are rarely Problem A issues. The majority of your significant arguments will stem from Problem B issues. The reason these will be so significant is because they are more closely tied to emotions. These are, however, the conversations and arguments that you should have. Disagreement is actually healthy and important. You, however, want to have healthy, loving disagreements. You want to be able to have conversations that can draw you closer to God and each other, and move your marriage forward. To do this, it is important to not allow Problem B issues to fester and grow because of the emotion attached. You will resolve these Problem B issues by learning to value the differences in each other rather than hoping they will go away.

Acknowledge Differences

So, how do you embrace the differences in each other? The first step is to acknowledge that they exist. That may seem like a silly and simplistic statement but it carries a lot of weight. The reality is we are limited in our perception of the world. We cannot experience what others experience.

Every experience we have is particular to us and colored by the other experiences we have. Because every experience we have is colored by our perceptions, experiences, and biases, it is easy to think others experience things the way that we do.

The first time we went to the Universal Theme Parks in Florida, we learned that our son loves thrill rides. Universal has some pretty spectacular ones. The rides are 3D extravaganzas in which you feel like you are actually participating in the adventures of the characters from the Universal movies. The Harry Potter rides are particularly fantastic. You feel like you're flying through the air, getting attacked by villains and dragons, and experiencing the locations familiar to fans of the movies. Our son couldn't get enough of these rides. Bryon thought the visual and sound effects made them far more intense than any rollercoaster.

After experiencing all of these phenomenal thrill rides, Bryon decided to take our son on the one rollercoaster he was tall enough to ride. Since he enjoyed the other rides so much, Bryon thought this would be a piece of cake. It wasn't nearly as scary as the other rides they had ridden. Bryon was trapped in his own context. For a seven year old boy, the sound and visual effects of the thrill ride brought him into a much loved movie. He felt like he was living out experiences he had only imagined before. A roller coaster is very different. In a rollercoaster you do not live out your fantasies of being a character in a movie. You only experience wind and speed and being jerked around by the different forces exerted on your body. While Bryon thought this would be equally as fun for our son, it was not. He explained at the end of the ride that he did *not* like rollercoasters. The problem was that Bryon was processing this through his particular experience and it turned out his experience was very different from our son's.

This is true of everything. Your experience is particular to you. But because you had that particular experience your whole life, you will often project that reaction and experience on others. We all do this. You will expect others to respond the way you would because it is natural to you. It is, however, not always natural or a first reaction by others to that same experience. To embrace your differences you need to acknowledge that they are there.

Identify Strengths

One of the more significant differences between the two of us is that when it comes to processing information, Bryon is an introvert and Jen is an extrovert. When faced with a problem or question of any kind, Bryon thinks it over in his head. By the time Bryon starts talking about an issue, he has thought it through very thoroughly and already come to a tentative conclusion. Bryon talks about a problem to test his conclusion and see what he has missed in the process. Jen processes information by talking about it. When Bryon starts talking about an issue, he has spent a significant amount of time thinking about it beforehand. When Jen starts thinking about a problem she starts talking about it.

This difference created some interesting conversations early in our marriage. Jen would start talking about a problem and come back to the same problem day after day as she processed the information. The problem would not be particularly vexing to her. She would merely be thinking about it. This was completely foreign to Bryon. Bryon would only spend that much time talking about a problem if it was weighing on him heavily and he could not come to a conclusion about the issue. He thought Jen was agonizing over a rather minor issue when she was just thinking about it and in the process of resolving it.

The way we process information has its unique strengths and weaknesses. Bryon is very decisive. He thinks things through on his own, makes a decision, and acts on it. Bryon keeps things moving forward. Bryon, however, can overlook issues because he only considers his point of view. Other opinions and ideas are never addressed because he didn't think about them.

Jen, on the other hand, is very good at collecting data. As she talks to people while she's thinking she gets their opinions and points of view. She incorporates all of these ideas and thoughts into her decision making process. Thus providing her with a bigger picture of the situation. Jen, however, can sometimes overthink an issue making her slower to act. All of the ideas and perspectives she sees can make it more difficult to choose a direction.

For us this is a perfect pairing. Jen helps Bryon make sure he's looking at situations from as many angles as possible to see a fuller picture. Bryon helps Jen settle on a decision and move forward.

We have learned that there are differences in how we process information. We have also learned that there are strengths that we don't share but when we apply our strengths together we can accomplish more than we would without each other.

What differences do you see in each other? What strengths does your spouse possess that you do not? Take some time this week and separately sit down and list out the differences you see in your spouse. Once you have written down those differences, write out the strengths and weaknesses you see. After that sit down together and read your list to each other. Then talk about how you can use each other's strengths to help each other and your marriage. You may be surprised to discover that your differences complement each other well.

Encourage Differences

Acknowledging differences and identifying strengths are important steps in embracing differences. This last point may, however, be the most important in strengthening your relationship. You need to encourage each other's differences.

As we discussed above, the tendency is for people to try to minimize differences in others. When dating, people are attracted to and focus on their similarities. Those similarities are important and are going to help your relationship stay strong. If you want a thriving, healthy marriage that will last a lifetime, you need to encourage how you and your spouse are different from each other. By encouraging one another's differences you are communicating that you value each other's individual identities not just your identity as a couple. This mutual encouragement will allow you to be your own person and your spouse to be their own person while simultaneously building a stronger marriage.

For us one of the significant differences comes from Bryon's affinity with the military. For Bryon, the military is fundamental to who he is. He grew up the child of an Army officer living on military bases for the first fourteen years of his life. At age 23 he enlisted in the Michigan Air National Guard, continuing a tradition of military service in his family that goes back generations. One of his ancestors was an English longbowman serving under King Henry VIII. The military is part of the core of who Bryon is.

The military has a unique subculture. There are things common to the military that are foreign to other professions and subcultures in the United States. We have had many conversations where there was an impasse because Bryon saw things fundamentally through his military mindset and Jen did not see things the same way.

Yet in spite of her unfamiliarity with many things about military culture, Jen supports Bryon's military career. As a National Guard family, this is different from active duty military families because Bryon's military career does not provide significant financial income for the family. We cannot rely on Bryon's military pay for our bills because he only works there one weekend a month plus another 20 - 30 days out of the year for special jobs or training.

Jen sacrifices a lot for what amounts to a part-time job for Bryon. He's away from home a lot. His job requires that he do work from home when he is off-duty. Currently, Bryon is serving as the Wing First Sergeant which requires him to effectively be on call 24/7.

Throughout all of this Jen does not only support Bryon's military career, she encourages it. When there is an opportunity for Bryon to do something that will help his military career she makes arrangements to take care of things at home so he can go. She encourages him to go to schools that will help him develop as an airman. She attends social events for the military because they are important to Bryon. In this way, Bryon can feel confident in himself because he knows that Jen values the things that are important to him simply because they are important to him. She encourages his differences.

Now that you've identified your differences and strengths, take time to discuss how you can encourage each other's differences in your marriage.

- Talk about ways in which you feel that your differences are encouraged.
- Share the ways you feel that your differences are not encouraged.
- Be open about the difficulties you face in being encouraging to each other's differences.

- Come up with a plan to be more encouraging.
- Notice when your respective differences are also your personal strengths, and in turn, strengths as a couple.
- Schedule a time three months from now to have this conversation again and see how you're both doing, how you're becoming more encouraging, and what you can do to improve.

Conclusion

Marriage is a unique and exciting relationship in which two people become one couple. It is tempting to believe that becoming one couple means becoming exactly alike. This could not be further from the truth. God created each of you as unique individuals. Marriage, becoming one couple, should be a process making you more the unique you that God created you to be, not less.

Two individuals becoming fully the person they were created by God to be makes for a strong couple. Like the persons of the Trinity who fulfill separate roles based on their unique identity, a husband and wife become a stronger couple when each is allowed to fully express their differences in a healthy relationship. Healthy, thriving individuals have healthy, thriving marriages.

The best way in a marriage to ensure that you both are able to become the individuals that God created you to be is focusing on and embracing each other's differences. When you both focus on helping your spouse be the unique individual God created them to be, you both will experience strength, love, and fulfillment in your marriage. To do this, (1) acknowledge your differences, (2) identify strengths, and (3) encourage each other's differences.

Action Steps:

Review the portions of this chapter titled "Identify Strengths" and "Encourage Differences." Discuss your answers to the questions contained in those sections.

CHAPTER 8

WHAT IS LOVE?

Love is confusing isn't it? One of the reasons it's so confusing is that it seems we really aren't sure what it is. The confusion about love has made it into all sorts of songs from country music such Eli Young Band's *Love Ain't*:

I may not know what love is girl, but I know but I know what love ain't

To Foreigner's classic rock anthem *I Want to Know What Love Is*:

I wanna know what love is
I want you to show me.

Perhaps most famously danced to at clubs around the world in Haddaway's 1993 hit *What Is Love*:

What is love?
Baby don't hurt me
Don't hurt me
No more

Admit it, by the end you were singing along weren't you?

The confusion about love has been preached by almost every pastor in every church. From the newest youth pastor to the most seasoned pastor getting ready to retire, they all have a sermon in their files that illustrates the confusion of how we use the word love to describe different feelings. We love pizza different from how we love our parents. We love sports teams different from how we love our children. We love our shoes differently from how we love our friends. We love our pets differently from how we love our spouse. Love is a confusing word.

If you've spent much time in church you've also heard that the New Testament was written in Greek. In those same sermons mentioned above each of those pastors will explain that Greek had three different words for love:

> Eros - romantic love, physical love, lust

> Phileo - brotherly love (most pastors can't help themselves but mention this is how the city of Philadelphia got its name)

> Agape - Godly love, unconditional love, self-sacrificing love.

While pastors will often overemphasize the differences between biblical Greek and modern English, the use of the word love in the Bible can be confusing.

Not only is the word love confusing because it means so many different things in English and in Greek, our culture has placed a unique emphasis on the experience of love in human relationships.

Feeling Love

The emotion defined as love is big business in America. We have learned to monetize love in almost every relationship. It starts as soon as we're born. When our daughter was born we were bombarded with coupons and advertising fliers trying to get us to buy all kinds of things for her. If you really love your baby you need to get them this custom, four-speed, hand-made, fully customizable, walker with educational toys around the rim to prepare them to walk, run, and therefore help them get into an ivy league graduate school.

Once you finish paying-off the toy that your infant won't use for the next 8 months because they can't even hold their head up yet you look at the calendar and see Mother's Day is almost here. If you really love your mom you'll buy her this hand-selected custom diamond-encrusted necklace proudly displaying the birthstones of all her children and grandchildren. The necklace weighs so much that your mom throws out her back every time she wears it. But that's okay. If you really love your mom you'll buy her a spa day to help her relax and a massage to work out that back pain.

It goes on and on. There are birthdays, anniversaries, graduations, Christmas, Valentine's Day, Father's Day, etc. Here in Michigan, we even have a bizarre holiday called Sweetest Day. Sweetest Day is the same as Valentine's Day, only it's in October because card companies and florists weren't making enough money off of Halloween. So enter a repeat of Valentine's Day several months later.

And here's the thing: we really do love all of those people. We feel deep affection for the important people in our lives. Of course, one of the people we have the strongest feelings of affection towards is the person to whom we're married. We feel a strong affection towards and desire for our spouse. You should feel this way about each other. Emotional love and connection is an important part of marriage.

For a long time passion and marriage was ignored or dismissed as unimportant in Christian circles. Historically, sex was connected with the original sin of Adam and Eve and, therefore, seen as something dirty or wrong. For a significant period of time in the history of the church, sex was viewed to be for procreation only. Any pleasure or passion connected with it was viewed as something connected with sin and temptation.

In reality, this is not what the Bible teaches about passion in marriage. The Song of Solomon is a poem extolling the virtues of passionate love in marriage. It is impossible to read the Song of Solomon honestly and not see how it encourages passionate sexual marriage relationships. Like many of Shakespeare's sonnets it is passionate, intimate, and poetically explicit.

Bottom line: you should feel passion for each other. You should feel the emotion labeled love towards each other. You should be attracted to each other. This is actually a very important part of your relationship, so much so that we have a whole chapter about it later in the book. Remember, however, that feelings ebb and flow. The feelings of passion you had towards each other during your engagement are different from the ones you felt on your wedding night which are different from the ones you felt during your worst fight.

Emotions ebb and flow because they are a reaction to your environment occurring before you have conscious thoughts about what is happening around you. The limbic system is a structure found roughly in the bottom center of your brain. One of the many functions of the limbic system is managing your emotional state. Your brain receives information about your environment through your five senses. These signals pass through your neurons to your brain and one of the first places to receive these signals is in your limbic system. From there it travels on to the different parts of your brain.

As one of the first parts of your brain to receive the messages about your environment, it responds before the other parts of the brain. In other words, the emotional part of your brain responds to your environment before the logical part does. In so doing, it causes your body to react to your environment before you think about it. The limbic system causes changes to your respiration, heart rate, and blood pressure. These biological responses then loop back to your brain, influencing how you think about and how you remember the events you experience.

For example, think about your last experience in a haunted house. At one point something jumped out at you from around a corner or out of a dark nook. Before you were able to process what just happened, you jumped. Perhaps you screamed. Your pupils dilated. Your heart rate and breathing increased. Your body was flooded with adrenaline. This is commonly called the fight or flight response. All of this happened before you were able to accurately assess the danger (or lack thereof) that you were in. You responded emotionally and physically before you were able to interpret logically.

So here's the point: your emotions are a preconscious response to stimulus. You respond to your environment emotionally before you think about what is going on. That means your emotions change based on your environment. One study has shown that judges are actually more harsh in their judgments when they are hungry.[28] Jen has seen this firsthand in the

---

[28] Kurt Kleiner, "Lunchtime Leniency: Judges' Rulings Are Harsher When They Are Hungrier", *Scientific American* (https://www.scientificamerican.com/article/lunchtime-leniency/?redirect=1, 2011), accessed May 28, 2019.

courtroom when it is getting closer to lunchtime. We've all been hangry, right?

It is, therefore, normal for your emotional state to change based on your circumstances. In fact, it is going to change and there is nothing you can do about it. That is why our emotions change so much. It is also why you cannot base your marriage on your emotional state. It is going to change.

Feeling romantic love towards each other is biblically important. In fact, it is essential. But it is not the only aspect of love that must be present in your relationship and cannot be the foundation of your relationship. Love, however, is not just how you feel. Love is also what you do.

Being Loving

Above we talked about how love is an emotion and emotions cannot be controlled. Yet, Jesus commands us to love:

This I *command* you - to love one another. (John 15:17, emphasis added)

"I give you a new *commandment*—to love one another. Just as I have loved you, you also are to love one another. (John 13:34, emphasis added)

Now one of the experts in the law came and heard them debating. When he saw that Jesus answered them well, he asked him, "Which commandment is the most important of all?" Jesus answered, "The most important is: 'Listen, Israel, the Lord our God, the Lord is one. Love the Lord your God with all your heart, with all your soul, with all your mind, and with all your strength.' The second is: 'Love your neighbor as yourself.' There is no other commandment greater than these." (Mark 12:28-31)

If love is an emotion and emotions cannot be controlled, how can Jesus command us to love? Is Jesus setting us up for failure?!

Of course not! This is why love is so confusing. The word describes so many different things. There is an emotion we experience that we call love but love is more than just that emotion. Love is an attitude one person has towards another. Love also consists of actions.

An Attitude of Love

As an attitude, we define love as thinking the best of and wanting the best for another person. The Bible gives us an obvious example of this in Jonathan and David, a strong, brotherly friendship rather than a marriage. Still, we learn so much about thinking the best of and wanting the best for another, which is applicable to marriage. Jonathan was the prince of Israel, the son of King Saul, and heir to the throne of Israel. David was a servant to King Saul, a military leader of Israel, and hired to play music that literally helped Saul chase away his demons. He was also God's choice to replace Saul as king of Israel and anointed by Samuel. David and Jonathan could have been opponents since Jonathan was next in line for the throne by human standards and David was a threat to Jonathan's rule. They were instead aligned in following God's will. During David's time serving Saul, Jonathan and David became best friends due to their strong faith in and hearts for God.

Over time, David lost favor with Saul, in no small part because he was a threat to Saul's throne and legacy. David turned out to be a very crafty tactician and military leader. "On every mission on which Saul sent him, David achieved success. So Saul appointed him over all of the men of war" (1 Samuel 18:5a). This, however, became an issue for Saul because the people were noticing that David was a more effective leader than Saul.

> The women who were playing the music sang,
> "Saul has struck down his thousands,
> but David his tens of thousands!"

> This made Saul very angry. The statement displeased him and he thought, "They have attributed to David tens of thousands, but to me they have attributed only thousands. What does he lack, except the kingdom?" (1 Samuel 18:7-8)

Clearly, Saul was no longer fond of his servant. In fact, Saul was so unhappy with David that the next day he threw his spear at him and tried to kill him twice.

Saul tried various ways to get rid of David but was unsuccessful every time. Finally, David came to Jonathan for help. "He came to Jonathan and asked, 'What have I done? What is my offense? How have I sinned before your father? For he is seeking my life!'" (1 Samuel 20:1). Jonathan promised to look into the issue for him.

Jonathan learned that Saul was, in fact, trying to kill David. Saul was so incensed by David that when Jonathan stood up for him Saul threw a spear at his own son. Jonathan then met David as they planned and helped him escape Saul. "Jonathan said to David, 'Go in peace, for the two of us have sworn together in the name of the Lord saying, 'The Lord will be between me and you and between my descendants and your descendants forever'"" (1 Samuel 20:42).

Jonathan wanted what was best for David. He faced great personal risk and sacrifice yet was loyal to his friend. Jonathan also thought the best of David. While Saul was convinced that David was trying to usurp his throne and destroy his legacy, Jonathan never believed that. Both Jonathan and David wanted and accepted God's will for David to be king of Israel one day. Jonathan always thought positively of David. Jonathan loved David.

Emotions ebb and flow based on our circumstances. We only have limited control of our feelings and therefore have only limited control over how we feel about people. Attitude, however, is completely under our control. You choose your attitude in any given situation. Your ability to choose your attitude is as true in marriage as anywhere else. Not only can you choose your attitude towards your spouse, *you are responsible for it*!

Your attitude will significantly determine your experience in marriage. If you want a thriving marriage that will last a lifetime, you must have the right attitude. First, you have to want what's best for them. You must choose to focus on their success and fulfillment. You must be willing to sacrifice your desires for their desires.

A common complaint for couples revolves around time spent with friends. Sometimes, one spouse will resent the time the other spends with friends. In such cases the resentful spouse is selfishly focused on their own wants and desires over those of the other. Yet sometimes, one spouse may need those relationships for their own fulfillment and emotional health. A loving attitude encourages those relationships without resentment or defensiveness.

We experienced this early in our marriage. Jen has a few good friends with whom she is very close. She wants to include them in almost every major event and important decision. The only things in which she does not include them are those that are private between the two of us. For a while, Bryon was frustrated with and a little jealous of these relationships. Often her friends would give the same advice about a situation as he did, but Bryon felt Jen gave their opinions more weight than his. Jen has maintained these friendships for over a decade, sometimes longer. Bryon does not have such relationships and did not understand their place in Jen's life. Once Jen explained why those relationships are important and Bryon saw that Jen continued to prioritize our marriage over those relationships, we were able to resolve the conflict.

This, of course, only works when it is mutual. Both spouses must have attitudes of love towards each other. In the example above, Jen had to consider the effect it was having on Bryon. Bryon had to equally want what was best for Jen.

The priority must still be your marriage. Together you must focus on what is best for the other. Inevitably this will require a willingness to sacrifice. It may require putting the kids to bed on your own occasionally or restructuring the budget to allow time out with friends. It may also require giving up nights out with friends occasionally to focus on the needs of your spouse, which is and must remain the more significant relationship to you.

Time with friends is only one example. The applications of this principle are endless. In any given moment or situation you choose your attitude. Are you choosing to want what's best for yourself or what's best for your spouse? Are you both together choosing what's best for you as a married couple? Are you effectively and consistently working towards the mission of becoming one? Are you fulfilling the priorities of Team Marriage and the others expressed in *Operation: Thriving Marriage*?

The other aspect of love as an attitude is thinking the best of a person. We call this presuming goodwill; we discussed this earlier and return to it because it is so important in love. We have talked to many people who are unhappy in their marriages. Many times, we have heard them give a laundry list of activities the other person has done to sabotage the marriage. Here's the reality: if you think your spouse is trying to cause problems for you and your marriage you will see every action through that lens. Little annoying habits, little things said or unsaid, small actions of little consequence all become major slights that eventually become irreconcilable differences. Things such as which way the toilet paper roll goes on the holder are matters of personal preference, not indications of compatibility in marriage.

Presuming ill will guarantees you will see everything your spouse does in a negative light. On the other hand, however, presuming goodwill will change your perspective entirely. When you presume goodwill, annoying habits and little actions that frustrate you aren't attempts to destroy your marriage but rather differences in preference or misunderstanding to be worked out.

There are myriads of things that happen in a marriage that can be frustrating or confusing. Little habits and presuppositions developed over your spouse's lifetime before you met are going to be different from yours.

When encountering something like this that triggers a negative emotion, stop and acknowledge the emotion you're experiencing. Then make a point to presume goodwill in the situation. Your husband or wife loves you. They are working to build a healthy thriving marriage with you that will last a lifetime. The action, whatever it was, was likely not intended to anger, frustrate, or upset you.

Then take a look at the action. How significant is the action? Is it a minor one-time event? Perhaps that is something you fix on your own with or without mentioning it. It's not a real issue. Is it a repeating pattern or a significant issue for you? Why does it bother you? Is it a presupposition of the way things ought to be? Is it an action that triggers negative emotions from a relationship in the past? If it is significant, take a moment to explain to them why this action bothers you. Tell them about the emotions tied to it and why it is important that the action changes. Work together to resolve the issue.

Jen has always had a good head for money management. Jen wanted to make sure that from the beginning, we had good plans to give, save, and spend. A month or so into our marriage, she asked Bryon to sit down and go over our last month's spending. Bryon took this as an attack on his spending habits; Jen was trying to see where they both were spending and how to cut costs and expenses to set us up to succeed in our mutual goals. We went over these monthly statements a couple more times until Bryon expressed his negative feelings. Jen was surprised that Bryon felt badly and expressed her feelings of wanting to be responsible and smart to help us as a married couple.

Through the whole process, Jen never presumed Bryon wanted to tank us financially speaking. Bryon's feelings were hurt because he presumed a personal attack, which Jen never intended. Bryon recognizes that he should not have presumed that Jen was attacking him personally. Instead, we have learned to presume that the other wants what's best for each other. We both know now to presume goodwill, and if we have questions or feel badly, we ask the other about it and discuss.

Love is more than a feeling or emotion. Love is attitude and action. An attitude of love is wanting what's best for the other and presuming goodwill in the other. This is the attitude Jonathan had towards David, a close friend, and it is also an attitude that spouses can have towards each other. This is the attitude that will lead you to have a healthy, thriving, lifelong marriage with your spouse.

Love in Action

Love is the *emotion* that launches and reinforces a marriage relationship. Love is the *attitude* that sustains a marriage. Love is the *actions* that maintain a marriage.

If you think about it, love in action is obvious. The actions of love communicate the reality of love. Telling your spouse that you love them is important. It's something they should hear from you everyday, but there is a limit to what words can communicate. The old adage is true: actions speak louder than words.

God knows this and, therefore, shows us his love far more than he tells us he loves us. One of the most dramatic examples of this is in the Book of Hosea. Hosea lives out a metaphor of how God loves his people in spite of their continuous rejection of him. In this lived out metaphor,

Hosea represents God and Gomer, Hosea's wife, represents God's people. Gomer is a prostitute. Gomer, however, is not a woman that was forced into prostitution and looking for a way out. She, rather, enjoys the lifestyle of a prostitute and the money and attention she gets from the men. She has no desire to remain faithful to Hosea. In spite of this, Hosea continues to pursue her. In spite of this, Hosea continues to welcome her into their home. In spite of this, Hosea continues to love her. Just like God continues to love us. "The LORD said to [Hosea], 'Go show love to your wife again, even though she loves another man and continually commits adultery. Likewise the LORD loves the Israelites although they turn to other gods" (Hosea 3:1-2a).

Of course the clearest example of God's love in action is Jesus. "For this is the way God loved the world: He gave his one and only Son" (John 3:16a). We like this translation because it more accurately communicates the intent of the original Greek. Many translations say "For God so loved the world" (NIV, ESV, NKJV). In modern English this communicates that God loved the world "so much" that he sent Jesus. While it's true that God loved us an awful lot to be willing to send Jesus, that's not the sense of the Greek. The original Greek more clearly communicates that sending Jesus is an act of love. Sending Jesus is what he did as love for us all. God's love is an action. Jesus going to his death for our sins and rising from the dead are incomprehensible actions expressing his love. The Holy Spirit's guidance, teaching, and reminders of Christ's teaching are actions of love. God's love is perpetual and without end, so his love expressed in action is also perpetual and without end.

Love is emotion. Love is attitude. Love is action.

What do your actions say about your love for your spouse? Better yet, what does your spouse say your action communicates about your love for them? Actions communicate different things to different people. Getting our son a gift no matter how inexpensive, communicates love to him. Our daughter, however, communicates love differently. To communicate love to her we need to spend time one-on-one with her. Gifts don't communicate as much to her.

During our honeymoon, we read *The 5 Love Languages* by Gary Chapman. It was very helpful for us. It helped us to see what actions communicate love to the other in a more clear way. Bryon's primary love language is physical touch. Hugs, kisses, and holding hands go a long way in communicating love to Bryon. Jen's, on the other hand, is more acts of service. This means that while Bryon is trying to communicate love by touch that is not always what it communicates to Jen. Taking time to clean up around the house or complete a task or chore that Jen normally does without asking, that communicates love. In the same way, Jen will do chores that Bryon normally does or take care of small tasks to communicate love to Bryon. Those messages, however, aren't as clear as a hug or a kiss or holding his hand, so Jen has adapted to express love to Bryon in these ways as well. It's been a learning curve for both of us, but well worth it.

Love is action. It is important for you to love your spouse through action. It is also important that you learn what actions communicate love for them. This is important for two reasons. First, you need to make efforts to do loving things that they will naturally see as loving. Second, you need to acknowledge the things they do that are intended to communicate love in a way that is less natural to you. When you mutually focus on this, it quickly increases how much love you share because you will both experience love not just from the way you naturally experience it but also from the way your spouse naturally expresses love. Commit to focusing on loving each other in both of these ways. It will build a thriving marriage.

Feel the Love

Let's circle back to emotional love now. At the beginning of this chapter, we talked about how we only have limited control of our emotions. The circumstances around us have a very significant impact on our emotions because we respond emotionally before we respond cognitively. Limited control, however, does not mean no control. In fact, while we have limited control over our emotions in marriage, the control we have is significant.

Our thoughts have a very strong impact over our emotions. Think about clowns for a moment. For some of you reading this, that thought elicited winsome feelings as you thought about face painting, or balloon animals, or too many people piling out of a little car. That thought made you feel happy. For others, you thought of creepy white-faced, red haired, sneering monsters. That thought made you feel fear. Either way, the thought made you feel something.

Let's apply that to your marriage. If you focus on loving attitudes and actions you will be thinking loving thoughts. These thoughts will affect your emotional experience. By thinking about loving your spouse you will feel more love towards your spouse.

There is another effect of being loving that will increase the emotional experience of love in your marriage. By acting loving towards each other you affect the context in which you live out your marriage. The loving attitude and actions you experience together will cause you to experience love through your senses. Your limbic system will process these experiences and produce the appropriate emotions before you are cognitively aware. Together, as you act loving towards each other, you will affect each other's emotions and create an environment for you both to feel more loving.

We say create the environment for this because we acknowledge that emotions are complex and a lot of things affect our experience. If one of you had a bad day at work, all the expressions of love may not cause a change in emotional experience because of other circumstances. You cannot control your spouse's emotions.

Conclusion

Love is confusing because the way we talk about it is confusing. The word carries more weight than those four little letters should truly manage. Since love is used in so many different ways to communicate so many different things, it is important to define love in marriage.

In marriage, there are three aspects of love. Love is the emotions you feel toward each other: the physical attraction, the romance, the affection. Love is the attitude you have towards each other. It is the desire for what's best for your partner and presuming goodwill in them. Love is the actions you take. You express your love to each other not only in words but in what you do every day.

You only have limited control of the love you feel. Your emotions are affected by the context in which you find yourself. You have complete control of your attitude and actions. What you think and what you do are solely controlled by your will. While you only have limited control of your emotions, what you think and the context you create for each other will affect your emotions. In this way, you have the ability to create the environment where you will feel more loving towards each other.

Action step:

Take some time today to discuss your thoughts about this chapter together.

- On a scale of one to ten, how loving do you feel towards your spouse today? Consider affection, physical attraction, and romance.
- How would you rate your attitude towards your spouse today?
  - o Have there been times when you did not want what's best for your spouse?
  - o How well have you presumed goodwill in the past week?
- Think about the last week. How loving were your actions?
- How loved have you felt in the past week?
- What adjustments can you make to feel more love towards your spouse?

CHAPTER 9

MORE THAN WORDS

It's no secret that communication is one of the most vital skills to building and maintaining a successful marriage. In fact, it might be the most important skill to building and maintaining a thriving marriage that lasts a lifetime. Any positive aspects we have developed in our marriage can be traced back to the communication skills we have developed. Any struggles we have had in our marriage are rooted in our lack of applying those skills at that time.

If communication is such an important aspect of marriage, then why did we wait until almost halfway through the book to start addressing it? Well, in a sense we have been dealing with it since the beginning of the book. Every chapter has conversation starters intended to help you focus on the theme of that chapter and discuss it together. The choice to discuss communication this late in the book, however, was very intentional.

Communication is a skill. It is actions that you take. Skills can be applied at any time in any situation, but for a skill to lead to the desired outcome it must be focused on the right outcome and rooted in the right values. In military operations, it's not enough to do the right things. The right things must be done in the right way to fulfill the mission. For the strategies in *Operation: Thriving Marriage* to be successful you must apply the right skills in the right way. You have to apply the skills necessary to fulfill your goal. Many marriages have a lot of communication but fail because the skills are not applied at the right time to the right issues.

Our goal is for you to have a healthy, thriving marriage that lasts a lifetime. That is why we've waited until this point to start discussing skill development. We, therefore, started this book discussing the nature of marriage and the values that will lead you to have the marriage that you want. We started by discussing the theology of marriage, defining marriage and the nature of marriage from a Christian perspective. Marriage was designed by God to help you experience and express his love. It exists to make you more holy. Then we talked about Team Marriage and love, the values that will lead to oneness and holiness in marriage. The rest of the book is going to focus on skills and actions rooted in the values and goal of oneness in marriage. The first is communication.

Wisdom in 90s Pop-Rock

Jen is a huge fan of 80s music. In her opinion, that decade was the pinnacle of American pop and rock music. She loves Madonna and Poison. Bryon is more of a fan of the alternative rock that developed in the 90s. The emotion of the music and the introspective lyrics speak to him. That transitional period in the late 80s and early 90s is a place they can both agree.

In that sweet spot, you will find the song "More than Words" by the band *Extreme*. It's a staple of any power ballad compilation. If you're not familiar with the song you should find it on YouTube and take a listen.

It's a great song, isn't it? We all know the sentiment that the band is communicating. We all want to hear the person we love say, "I love you", but hearing the words isn't enough. Truly communicating the love we feel and want to feel from our spouse requires more than words. We want to know we are loved without having to hear the words. In a relationship of love, communication is so much more than words.

Defining Communication

Like marriage and love, one of the key struggles with communication stems from an unclear definition of communication. Our favorite definition actually comes from Bryon's high school humanities class. In that class, communication was defined as a message by someone to someone else for some purpose. The great thing about this definition is that it applies to all forms of communication. The point in humanities class was to teach us that all forms of art are communication. To truly appreciate a sculpture, a painting, a song, a poem, a short story, a novel, a TV show, a movie, or a play, it is important to think about it as a form of communication. It is a message by the artist to the audience for a purpose.

Message

Let's break down that definition. The first aspect is the message. The message is the content of the communication. In every act of communication there are at least three messages. The first is the intended message of the sender. This is the thoughts the sender wishes to convey to the receiver. The second is the medium of the communication. The medium of the message is very complex and encompasses all the aspects of every form of communication. For our purposes here, we are going to focus on interpersonal verbal communication (typical of every couple) and purposefully exclude the various forms of art and written communication. That latter communication is a book in and of itself.

The medium of the message, of course, includes words spoken, but it is far more than words. The messenger (the sender) is the medium. When you communicate, everything about you is part of the message. Your body language is part of the message. Your tone of voice is part of the message. The role you play in the relationship is also a part of the message. The same words, tone and body language communicate something different from a spouse than they do from a parent or friend.

Bryon was recently talking about this subject with one of the pilots with whom he works. This particular pilot is a very large man. He is incredibly tall with broad shoulders. It's amazing he actually fits in the cockpit of the A-10 he flies. The man is so large his callsign (nickname given to a new pilot by other pilots in the unit) is Tree. One of the things that Tree has learned is that his size affects the message he is trying to communicate. Being such a large man he can be very intimidating. The medium muddies the message the sender is trying to send. As such, Tree makes a point to sit much of the time when he is talking to someone. Sitting down changes how he is perceived by the people to whom he is speaking. This subtle change allows him to more effectively communicate the message he intends to send.

Of these aspects of communication, the medium is the part over which you have the most control. We will spend a lot of time talking about the medium to help you communicate better. It is important to remember, however, the medium is not the message. The message you form in your head is never going to perfectly be the message in the medium. The medium is full of limiting factors that cloud the message you intend to send. The goal is to do everything possible to mitigate the limiting factors of the medium. That is what Tree does when he sits down to talk to people.

The third message is the message the receiver comprehends. The message the receiver comprehends is not always the same message the sender intends. There is a phrase we use in the Air Force that is probably used a lot of other places, too, in order to describe this reality: message sent was not message received.

The experience of the receiver drastically affects how they perceive the message. This includes both the experience in the particular moment and all the life experiences that preceded that moment. For example, a husband watching TV downstairs hears a strange noise coming from the bedroom upstairs. He yells upstairs, "What was that noise?" His wife was in the bedroom and she hears her husband yelling. Her first thought might be, "Why is he yelling at me?" For the husband this was a simple question looking for information. The increased volume of the medium was necessary to ensure the message could be heard by his wife. For the wife, however, the increased volume communicated agitation or perhaps anger. Message sent was not message received.

The above is an example of how the receiver's experience in the moment affects the message received. Here is an example of life experience affecting the message received. Growing up, Bryons' family teased each other a lot. It was one of the ways they communicated love to each other. Teasing, joking, trash-talking, all these were ways Bryon's family shared love in their family. When we were dating, Bryon would tease Jen. At one point, Jen, fed up with Bryon's antics, finally said, "Why are you being mean to me?" You see, Jen's family did not communicate in the way Bryon's did. When Bryon would tease Jen, she didn't hear love and affection. She heard unmerited criticism. Message sent was not message received.

Fortunately we have both grown since then. Jen has learned that Bryon's teasing is just a silly way to communicate affection and we now banter back and forth quite a bit. Bryon has learned to be more aware of the situation and learned how to tease in a way that communicates love to Jen. We have mitigated the limiting factors of our past and modified the medium of the message to communicate better with each other.

Sender & Receiver

Communication is a message by someone to someone else for some purpose. We have discussed the message as part of our definition of communication. Let's look at the "by someone to someone else" part of our definition. We touched on this a little in the section above. The "by someone" is the sender and the "someone else" is the receiver.

For our purposes these are husband and wife. The sender and receiver are you. Let's go back to the beginning of the book and remember what marriage is. Marriage is two individuals becoming one couple. The important thing to note here is that while you are one couple, you have not lost your individuality. You are still you. You are still unique. You carry everything with you that you always have. All of these facets influence your communication. And all of this is true of your spouse as well. Both of you remain unique individuals with unique histories and points of view.

Every person brings limiting factors (LIMFACs) into every instance of communication. These LIMFACs result from what makes you unique. They are caused by many different facets of who you are.

LIMFACs come from your presuppositions. Presuppositions are universal to the human condition. We all presume many things in life. We need these presuppositions to function in life. Imagine if every morning you had to think whether or not gravity would work the same way as it did yesterday. Getting out of bed would be a whole new adventure. Imagine if every time you went to sit in a chair you had to verify that it was a chair and would hold you up. You might have much stronger legs and back from all the times you chose to just stand and not risk it.

OK, granted these are silly examples of presuppositions but while presuppositions are universal, not all presuppositions are the same. Bryon experiences this a lot when talking to people about leadership and people development. As the son of an Army officer, Bryon grew up in a very leadership focused environment. This environment has extended into adulthood for him as a Senior Noncommissioned Officer in the Air Force. Through his entire life, he has been indoctrinated into a particular way of viewing leadership and people development. A very particular set of presuppositions has developed from that experience. Bryon presumes a lot of things about how organizations and people should function. When talking with other members of the military the shared experience and presuppositions make conversations about leadership and people development very easy.

As a pastor, Bryon often has conversations about leadership and people development in the context of church. In these contexts the military presuppositions regarding leadership and people development are not shared. While there are shared principles the language and presumed activities are not shared. He finds communicating about leadership and people development with other pastors much more difficult because of the differing presuppositions. Bryon's military presuppositions are LIMFACs that he must mitigate when communicating with other church leaders.

In seminary Bryon was taught to think about presuppositions like your big toe. Everyone has a big toe. Your big toe is essential for walking. No one thinks about their big toe until they stub it on a table or someone steps on it. Then they take efforts to protect it so it doesn't get hurt again.

Everyone has presuppositions. Presuppositions are essential to functioning in life. No one thinks about their presuppositions until something challenges them. Then they take efforts to resolve the challenge they're facing.

Your presuppositions are LIMFACs because they affect the message you form in your mind as the sender and how you perceive the message as the receiver. For effective communication, you as a couple need to identify the presuppositions creating LIMFACs and develop plans to mitigate those LIMFACs. For instance, it is well known that the military speaks in acronyms. Bryon often presumes that these acronyms are universal. Of course, in reality, they are not. This creates a LIMFAC in our communication. To mitigate this LIMFAC, Bryon does his best to use whole words and phrases when talking to Jen or defines acronyms when using them. Jen knows that Bryon thinks in acronyms and that a LIMFAC in communication is that she does not know them all. To mitigate the LIMFAC, Jen does her best to learn the common acronyms that Bryon uses and instead of getting frustrated when he uses an acronym she doesn't know, she instead asks for clarification.

Presuppositions are not limited to the words we use. Presuppositions extend to every aspect of our lives. They include how we say things. They include body language and tone of voice. They are particularly relevant to our individual world view. All of these create LIMFACs. All of these LIMFACs can be mitigated. As a couple it is important to identify them together and mitigate them.

Identifying and mitigating LIMFACs starts with a presupposition that together you will work on this. Alway presume good will and acknowledge in communication when you have encountered a LIMFAC and that together you will mitigate it.

The Purpose

The last and potentially most overlooked aspect of communication is the purpose. Why are you communicating in the first place? Is this conversation about sharing information about what's going on with the kids? Are you looking for advice about something? Are you trying to convince your spouse of something? Did your spouse do something that hurt your feelings that you want to resolve? Are you seeking forgiveness? Are you trying to communicate that you forgive them? Are you trying to connect emotionally? Are you simply trying to express love? What is the purpose of the communication?

Identifying the purpose of your communication affects the medium of the message. If you are simply sharing information about your kids, then the words, action, and tone should be different from seeking advice on how to deal with an issue that happened with them while your spouse wasn't there. If your goal is simply to share information and your spouse is going into problem solving mode the message sent is not the message received. If the message sent is not the message received then do something about it. Change the message in the medium. Change the words you're using, adjust your tone, change your body language. You need to become very self aware. Be aware of every aspect of what you're doing and adjust the medium to affect how the message is received.

Knowing the purpose also affects the message you want to send and how far you want to press the conversation. One of the ways Bryon often tries to connect with Jen is to talk to her about the cases she is working on. Recently she was working on a case that was very frustrating. The court staff was not acting as they are supposed to, resulting in a conflict between Jen and one of the members of the court staff. Her opposing counsel was not reading the paperwork filed on the case and stonewalling in negotiation. The case was using up a lot of Jen's bandwidth and burning up her emotional reserves. Bryon brought up the case after dinner. We talked briefly about the case, then Jen asked to talk about something else. Because the goal was to connect with Jen, Bryon changed the topic immediately. Pursuing that topic any further would have been counterproductive. If, however, the conversation had been about something else with the purpose of resolving an issue, such as the destination of a family vacation, then Bryon should have continued the conversation mitigating the LIMFACs that were preventing the message from being received.

Conclusion

Communication is a message by someone to someone else for some purpose. It is not limited to the words that are said. Communication involves every aspect of the person sending and the person receiving the message. Everyone walks into moments of communication with a unique point of view and unique history that creates limiting factors to the effectiveness of the communication. It is your job, whether sender or receiver, to mitigate those limiting factors the best you can. Being aware of the purpose of the communication is equally important. The purpose will determine the message, the medium, the extent of the conversation, and how it is received.

Action step:

- This week, take some time to list the LIMFACs you are aware of in your communication and the LIMFACs you notice in your spouses communication.
- Take time to share your lists. Note the similarities and differences in your lists.
- Develop a plan to mitigate at least one of each of your LIMFACs.

CHAPTER 10

CAN I HEAR YOU NOW?

In the early 2000s there was a popular cell phone commercial featuring a guy walking around carrying a cell phone asking the person on the other end, "Can you hear me now?" He would wait a couple of seconds then cheerfully respond, "Good!" That poor actor became so identified with that role that the next time we saw him was in another cell phone commercial. Hopefully he got paid well.

The point of the commercial was to communicate that users of that service would have good coverage in even the strangest places. Back then cell phone usage was just taking off and service was isolated to urban centers and spreading from there. This company was arguing that their service was available in more locations than anyone else. They had created a service where I could hear you anywhere if you were using their service. They had mitigated LIMFACs that other companies had not to improve communication.

In the last chapter, we defined communication as a message by someone to someone else for some purpose. We talked about the elements of the definition: the message, sender, receiver, and purpose. We also discussed limiting factors (LIMFACs) that hinder communication. In this chapter, we're going to focus on common LIMFACs of senders. We will provide information to help you mitigate those LIMFACs and improve your ability to send your message in a way that will be received.

Speaking to be Heard

The message you send is irrelevant if it is sent in a way that cannot be heard or understood. When watching movies or TV shows showing police or military talking on their radios, have you ever wondered why they say niner, instead of nine for the number 9? This developed with the phonetic alphabet in the early days of radio to ensure clear communication across different languages and cultures. In German the word for no is *nein*, pronounced nine. Imagine the confusion that would result of sender and receiver were confused about whether the message was the number 9 or no. Niner, resolved the problem.

The concept is true in all communication. If you want the receiver to understand your message, you have to communicate in a way that they will understand. You have to speak so that they can hear you. It is your responsibility to mitigate as many LIMFACs as possible to ensure your message is getting through loud and clear. Successfully accomplishing your mission to have a thriving marriage requires that you adapt your sending style in a way that the receiver, your spouse, can hear you, not expecting them to adapt to your style.

It is helpful here to consider how important God considers the way you speak. James, the brother of Jesus, discussed this in his letter. It is one of the more popular texts in Scripture regarding speech. The full passage is found in James 3:1-12. Here we will refer to some of the key points. Perhaps the easiest and most frequent way we sin is with our words. "For we all stumble in many ways. If someone does not stumble in what he says, he is a perfect individual, able to control the entire body as well" (James 3:2). How many times have you said something and immediately thought, "I wish I could take that back"? Words are one of the first ways we react to any situation. As we start feeling strong emotions, we use *words* to express what we're feeling. You can see a perfect example of this if you attend a live sporting event. Fans cheer their team, boooo the opposing team, and ridicule the officials for calls against their team. The emotions of the moment lead people to vocalize their experience. The same is true in your marriage. There are times when you look at each other and can't help but express your love and affection in words. Equally, in times of anger and frustration, you express yourself in words. "Think how small a flame sets a huge forest ablaze. And the tongue is a fire! The tongue represents the world of wrongdoing among the parts of our bodies. It pollutes the entire body and sets fire to the course of human existence—and is set on fire by hell" (James 3:5b-6).

Your words can be a major LIMFAC to communication. You must, therefore, choose your words carefully. Every word you say carries weight. Ephesians 4:29 says, "You must let no unwholesome word come out of your mouth, but only what is beneficial for the building up of the one in need, that it may give grace to those who hear." Some words carry greater weight than others depending on the personal history of the people in the conversation. The words "calm down" are a great example here. Parents often tell their children to calm down because the children need to calm down. They are either playing too loud or too rambunctiously for the space or they are letting their emotions control them in an unhealthy way. This is a perfectly acceptable thing to say to children. It is not, however, always the best thing to say to a spouse, however well-meaning you are. When an adult is starting to express strong negative emotions, it is often a bad idea to tell them to calm down, because it comes across as patronizing. "Calm down!" is what you say to children, not an adult. The adult may need to calm down, but saying it like that won't work. Other words need to be chosen because of the weight that "calm down" carries due to how it's been used.

Jen is a State Court Administrative Office approved mediator in the State of Michigan, so she facilitates mediations between competing parties and their attorneys to resolve legal disputes. One of her mediator mentors told the story of how he, early on in his mediation career, told a woman on one side of the issue to "calm down." She clearly felt dismissed and like her emotions and position did not matter; she and her attorney almost left and mediation efforts almost failed. He said that this tactic to tell anyone to "calm down" inevitably fails and often ramps up the negative, uncontrolled emotions even more. Even when an adult needs to calm down, another tactic must be taken to get them to calm down.

While telling someone to "calm down" is a good example, it is even more important regarding the use of words that are insulting, demeaning, or hurtful. It is never ok to use words that are intentionally painful when talking to each other. It doesn't matter what you're feeling or what happened. Spiteful, vengeful, hurtful, words are unloving and sinful. When tempted to talk in this way, you need to develop a strategy to keep it from happening. This requires self-awareness. When your emotions start to flare, what happens to you? Do you grit your teeth? Does your face flush? When Bryon starts to get angry he can feel his heart start beating harder and faster. He also starts breathing hard and gets jittery. When that happens, he knows his emotions are flaring. He, therefore, knows he needs to think very carefully about his word choice to make sure the words he is using are the right words for the situation.

Equally important is learning the words that carry extra weight with your spouse that may not carry the same weight with you. You both have different histories and experiences. Words, therefore, carry different connotations for you. This is something that takes a long time to learn. Pay attention to each other's reactions. When a word triggers a reaction, explore that together. Discuss why that word triggers that kind of emotion and learn how to work through that. Equally important is telling each other when words carry a lot of weight for you. Remember to presume good will. Your spouse is not trying to hurt your feelings. If that word or phrase is a problem for you, explain to them why. These conversations will be great ways to grow closer to each other if you take the time to share fully and listen carefully.

It's not just the words that are important. Proverbs 15:1 says, "A gentle response turns away anger, but a harsh word stirs up wrath." Your tone can be a significant LIMFAC to communication. It is important to use the tone that communicates the message you are trying to convey. This can be a lot trickier than it sounds. It requires you to listen closely to yourself as you speak. Many people are very unaware of the tone they use when they speak. They just talk. This is a common conversation we have with our children. When they're talking to us they can have a tone that is inconsistent with their goal. It can come across as whiney or condescending. For them, they have picked up the tone that their friends often use in different conversations. They are not even aware of the tone that they are using. They have not learned to listen to themselves when they talk. Unfortunately, many adults haven't developed this skill either. They aren't aware of the tone of their voice when they talk, nor have they mastered how to control it. This is another skill that can be learned, so don't give up!

We have a friend that teaches about leadership and volunteer development. When she teaches about tone she talks about something she calls the "butter voice." Your "butter voice" is the voice you use when you're asking your mom to pass the butter at the dinner table. As a child, you probably learned quickly how to appropriately ask your mom to pass the butter at the table. You learned the tone that was appropriate. Asking for butter should carry a relaxed, sweet, and kind tone. As an adult, you need to learn what tone is appropriate for every situation. Most of the time as mentioned in the Proverbs passage above, your butter voice is going to be more effective when discussing tough issues with each other.

Tough Conversations

The way you handle tough conversations can make or break your relationship. Effective communication is vital to every aspect of your marriage. It is probably, however, more important in the tough, difficult conversations than anywhere else. This is because of how emotions impact memory and behavior. We talked in an earlier chapter about how the limbic system works and how emotions are felt before thoughts are formed. One of the impacts of this is that events connected to strong emotions become more cemented while memories with less emotional content do not linger as long. This is part of the reason people experiencing traumatic events may suffer from PTSD. It is also why you probably don't have much trouble remembering your wedding day or your first kiss. You probably remember them vividly because of the emotions associated with those events.

Tough conversations are often highly emotionally charged. Because of the emotions attached, how you handle such conversations will have a lingering effect on you and your relationship. It is, therefore, very important that you successfully navigate those conversations. David prayed, "Set a guard, O LORD, over my mouth; keep watch at the door of my lips" (Psalm 141:3). David understood the impact that verbal communication has. In this section, we will focus on the sending aspect of the conversation; in the next chapter, we will discuss overcoming the LIMFACs on the receiving side of the communication.

When facing a difficult conversation, it is important to remember the *purpose* of the conversation. The goal of the tough conversation is to resolve an issue or conflict to strengthen your relationship. The goal is *never* to win an argument or prove that you're right. You could win every argument and be right every time and quickly be divorced. Before we married, a long-time medical malpractice defense litigator gave Jen this advice: your argumentation skills from law school are like a samurai sword. Never use them in your marriage. Like a sword, words and tone during an argument can cut deep, sometimes leaving permanent damage. As such, the words you use and tone you choose must reflect the goals of the conversation: jointly overcoming the obstacle (disagreement) and bringing you closer together. So, in an argument with your spouse, do you want to be right or do you want to be close? Use the opportunity to understand each other better and grow closer to each other.

With that said, we're not naive. We are well aware that it is easier to write a chapter about this than it is to live this out. We also make no claims to being perfect at this. Not all of our tough conversations go the way they should. That's why forgiveness is so important. Our tough conversations are better now both because we have learned to incorporate these skills in our relationship and we are also quick to forgive each other when we fail to implement the skills we discuss in this book.

When dealing with tough conversations, the book *Preparing Couples for Love and Marriage: A Pastor's Resource* gives this advice:

> Speak in a way that makes it easier for one's partner to listen. This isn't about simply "getting one's feelings out." Careless words send a hurtful message: "Getting something off my chest is more important to me than you or our relationship." That triggers defensiveness and makes it far less likely that the speaker will be heard.[29]

Remember the goal: resolve the issue and grow closer. You won't do this if you just unload everything on your spouse.

It may be helpful to imagine it like this. Recently we were watching the TV show *Insane Pools* on HGTV. In this episode, the team was building a pool in Utah. The host and designer was fascinated by the rocks they were using. Normally, the team builds pools in Florida. The rock they use for

---

[29] *Preparing Couples for Love and Marriage: A Pastor's Resource*, 42.

the hardscape mostly comes from the Smoky Mountains in Tennessee. The rock they used in Utah was from the Rocky Mountains and much denser than the rock from Tennessee. In Utah, the rock was delivered by dump truck and unceremoniously dumped on the ground. This would have been disastrous for the less dense rock from Tennessee. The softer Tennessee rock would crack or perhaps shatter from such treatment. Tennessee rock is delivered on pallets via flatbed, forklifted off, and gently put in place by a skilled crane or excavator operator.

"Getting it off your chest" is like delivering rock in Utah. You unceremoniously dump everything out and let your partner sort through the mess. You see the problem: your stuff hasn't broken, but it is dense and may hurt your spouse. Instead, as you share your feelings with your spouse, do so like delivering Tennessee rock. Place it carefully before them and together look at it and figure out how it fits into the beautiful relationship landscape that you are building together.

This doesn't mean repressing your feelings. That is equally disastrous to your relationship. It will only build feelings of resentment and create distance between the two of you. Rather, lovingly share what is going on inside of you in a way that allows you both to explore the feelings and work through strategies to deal with the issues at hand. Jesus instructs us to lovingly confront others and this includes our spouse. Jesus said, "If your brother sins go and show him his fault when the two of you are alone. If he listens to you, you have regained your brother" (Matthew 18:15). Confrontation is not condemnation. Do not marinate in bad feelings; rather work through the feelings and issues together.

Remember the mission when choosing your words and tone with each other. You are in this together and your word choice and tone should reflect that in your communication. Choose words and a tone that will encourage an open non-defensive posture. Avoid phrasing that creates a combative environment. This will make it easier for your spouse to hear the message you're sending without getting caught up in the way the message is being sent.

Conclusion

Communication is a message by someone to someone else for some purpose. The message you send to your spouse is irrelevant if they cannot receive it. It is up to you to send the message in a way that they can receive it. There are many LIMFACs that you have to overcome to send your message. Two ways to mitigate the LIMFACs of communication are to consider your word choice and tone. To effectively communicate, focus on ensuring your word choice and tone to add to rather than detract from the message that you are sending.

The importance of effective communication is amplified when dealing with tough conversations. This is because the emotion involved in these conversations increases their impact on your relationship. To successfully navigate tough conversations, remember the goal is to resolve the issue and grow closer together. Communicate your emotions carefully without unloading on your spouse. Make sure your tone and word choice help to maintain an open, non-defensive posture.

Action step:

Think of a recent tough conversation that you have had. Together discuss how you presented your emotions to each other.

- Did you unload your emotions on each other or lovingly present them to each other?
- What about your tone and word choice?
- Did they help create an open non-defensive environment?
- What could you have done better?

CHAPTER 11

SHHHHHHHH

"Being heard is so close to being loved that for the average person they are almost indistinguishable." - David Augsberger, *Caring Enough to Hear and Be Heard*

The most important skill you will ever develop in life is listening. There is no relationship in the world that can't be improved by better listening. The most important skill in business is listening. It doesn't matter how amazing your product or service is; if you don't listen to your customer you will never sell it. The most important skill in leadership is listening. It doesn't matter if you have a great vision or plan that will benefit the whole team; if you don't listen to your team you will never solve the problems your team is facing. The most important skill in parenting is listening. It doesn't matter that you are right or that you have more experience; if you don't model listening to your children, they will never listen to you. The importance of listening cannot be overstated. It is the most important skill in life.

Jen's first internship with a judge was during Summer 2001. It was in a criminal courtroom where felonies were prosecuted and many of the defendants were dangerous. These defendants were shackled and guarded by deputies. There was a defendant who was on trial for and ultimately convicted of first-degree murder for scalding a two-year-old girl to death in a bathtub. He was a big, towering guy. Defiant. Angry. The sheriff's deputies who escorted this defendant into and out of the courtroom sometimes struggled to keep him under control. This, of course, affected the safety of everyone in the courtroom. Because of the trouble the deputies had with him, Jen was instructed to move from her usual spot near where the defendant would walk into the courtroom to a place farther away. It was important that she listened carefully to the deputies. It wasn't enough to just move. She had to move to the right place in the courtroom. It wasn't a time to think or evaluate. It was a time to listen. Had she not listened, she could have put herself and everyone in the courtroom in significant danger.

As important a skill as listening is, it is often a hard skill to develop. If you really think about it, listening is counterintuitive. Listening goes against our nature. It is the opposite of what we truly desire. Thanks to sin, our nature is selfish. Since the fall, all humanity has been self-focused. The original temptation to "be like God" played on the root of selfishness. Cain's murder of Abel was selfish. He was jealous that God accepted Abel's sacrifice over his. This sin continues on and on throughout the Book of Genesis and the entire Bible. Sin is *selfishness*. When we focus on ourselves without thought or concern about other people, this world God has given us, or God himself, we are being selfish. We sin.

Our sinful nature is a significant LIMFAC to communication and developing good listening skills. A core desire in all people is to be heard, understood, and validated. We do not need to have the listener agree with us, but merely take time to hear, understand, and value us. This is highlighted by David Augsberger's quote that opened this chapter. When we feel heard, we feel loved. It is, therefore, natural for us to work at the goal of being heard. We desperately want to be heard so we use every tool in our toolbox to accomplish that goal. It is not sinful to want to be heard; it is sinful to do so by trampling others to serve ourselves and then choose to not "hear" and understand others.

Dietrich Bonhoeffer also equated Jesus' command to love with listening. He wrote, "The first service that one owes to others in the fellowship consists in listening to them. Just as love to God begins with listening to his Word, so the beginning of love for the brethren is learning to listen to them."[30] This is certainly applicable to your marriage. To have thriving marriages that last a lifetime we need to overcome our sinful nature and build the skills necessary to express love to each other. Thankfully, the first part was taken care of for us. Jesus' death and resurrection defeated sin in

---

[30] Dietrich Bonhoeffer, *Life Together*, (London: SCM Press Ltd, 1949), 52, Kindle Edition.

the world and in our lives. Now our part is to develop the skills that will express love to each other. Part of expressing love is listening well. We need to develop good listening skills.

Listening Competency

Every career field in the Air Force has a Career Field Training and Education Plan (CFETP). The CFETP describes the training milestones expected of airmen at different points in their career. Upon graduation from Basic Military Training (BMT), every airman has a skill level of one: a helper. A one level airman understands basic airmanship and can do very simple tasks with supervision. They are not yet qualified to do anything within their career field. Upon graduation from BMT, airmen go to technical school to learn how to do their job. Upon graduation from technical school airmen are awarded a three level. At that point, they are capable of doing basic tasks within their career field with supervision. Bryon would tell airmen when they graduated tech school that he didn't expect them to be loggies (Logistics Planners). He expected them to speak loggie. He would teach them to be loggies. Throughout their military career, airmen would enhance their skills and become more proficient in their career field.

The CFETP for each career field has a task list describing the skills an airman needs in that career field along with the necessary competency for each skill level. For instance, logistics planners are responsible for planning how a unit will send people from their base to a deployed location. A three level loggie "can identify basic facts and terms about the subject."[31] A five level loggie "can identify relationships of basic facts and state general principles about the subject."[32] A seven level loggie "can determine step by step procedures for doing the task."[33] As you can see, the Air Force has defined the levels of competency necessary for each skill.

Our daughter studies martial arts and recently earned her black belt. The belt system in martial arts is very similar to the Air Force career

---

[31] *AFSC 2G0X1 Logistics Plans Career Field Education and Training Plan*, (Department of the Air Force, 2019), 23.

[32] ibid.

[33] ibid.

development system. Everyone starts as a white belt: brand new to martial arts with no competency in any of the skills. As they move on in the colored belts they slowly become more competent. By the time they earn their red belt, the last color before black, they have demonstrated high competency in the basics of their art. Upon attaining their black belt, the students have proven they are competent in the basics of the style and are now ready to move on to more advanced skills.

Listening Skill Development Path

Listening is just like the skills in Air Force career fields or martial arts. There are levels of competency. Through effort, practice, and training, we all can become better listeners. In the Air Force, there is a stopping point in career skill development. Once an airman has received their nine level they are considered completely competent in their career field. Martial arts is a little different in this. Skill development never stops in martial arts. Practitioners of martial arts believe in continual process improvement. They practice their martial art perpetually, believing they can always improve their skills. Listening, in this case, is more like martial arts. No one is a perfect listener. Our listening skills can always improve. That being said, we're going to propose an Air Force style skill description to provide a framework to talk about listening skills. Remember, however, listening is something that must be practiced consistently and will consistently improve throughout the rest of your life if you are consistent and unfailing in putting effort towards improvement.

In the book *The Life You've Always Wanted*, John Ortberg describes the difference between training and trying. Trying is working hard to get better. Trying lacks strategy and focus. Trying to get better at a skill expends a lot of energy but leads to little or no results. Training is trying with discipline and purpose. Discipline can be defined as *doing what I can do today so I can do tomorrow what I can't do today*. Trying with purpose is trying with a goal in mind.

Members of the US Military are expected to be leaders at whatever level they find themselves. Throughout his career, Bryon was trying to be a good leader. He read books, attended training, and made and implemented plans. Bryon was trying hard. He put forth a lot of effort and was making some improvement. But he was trying, not training. He wasn't even sure how to train himself to be a better leader. This changed when Bryon attended the US Air Force Senior NCO Academy - Advanced Leadership Experience (SNCOA-ALE). While there, the skills necessary to be a good leader were defined. Tasks to develop these skills were discussed and demonstrated. Opportunities to work on these skills were provided and feedback was given. When Bryon returned from SNCOA-ALE, he implemented the practices he learned and began to train himself to be a better leader. Like listening, leadership is a continuous development process. In the next few paragraphs, we hope to provide you tasks that you can do today to help you train to be a better listener tomorrow.

Level 1: Apprentice

Bryon's grandmother, an amusing old southern belle we called Mamma Dee, offered this little gem to her grandchildren, "You should listen twice as much as you speak. That's why God gave you two ears and one mouth." While that may not have been original with Mamma Dee, the thought behind it is true. We are born with the ability to listen. Don't believe us? Spend some time with a toddler. Everything you say can and will be repeated, at the most embarrassing moment possible. We're all born knowing the basics of listening. The problem is that as we get older more and more things vie for our attention. We don't focus on listening because of all the noise around us. We're distracted by the sights and sounds going on around us. We're distracted by the thoughts in our heads. We're all like the dog in the movie *Up!* because there are, indeed, squirrels everywhere.

Distractions are significant LIMFACs to listening. Apprentice listeners learn to mitigate distractions to listening. The first step here is to identify what distracts you from listening. A common listening distraction is television. Our brains are designed to key in on movement. The constant movement on televisions is a significant LIMFAC to listening that is easily mitigated.

Most nights after the children go to bed, we watch TV to unwind. As we sit there watching TV our minds are sorting through the events of the day. Often something important will occur to one of us during the show that we want to discuss. The TV is a distraction to be mitigated. So that we can listen better to each other, we pause the television show using our DVR or streaming service. The LIMFAC thus mitigated allows us to listen better.

Television is not the only distraction. It is impossible for us to know the things that distract you. Here are a few common distractions and our suggestions to mitigate them. Use this list as an illustration to help you identify the things that distract you and develop strategies to mitigate them.

- Children: Children can be a major distraction. They interrupt when you are talking. They make noise. They bicker. They fuss. When you find yourself distracted by children ask if you can continue the conversation after they go to bed. If the conversation is urgent and must happen immediately, try going outside for a walk.
- Cell phones: The incessant buzzing, chirping, and ringing make it difficult to focus. It's hard to resist looking at that text or who is calling. When having a conversation together, turn them off completely. Putting them on silent or in another room doesn't work very well because they often still vibrate or if connected to a smart watch will still distract you in some fashion.
- Thoughts of work: This is perhaps the most pernicious distraction and most difficult to mitigate. We haven't found a way to shut off, pause, or remove thoughts. The only way we have been able to mitigate this LIMFAC is through disciplined focus on what the other person is saying and the refusal to mentally wander into thoughts of work. The next skill is the best mitigating factor that we have found.

Level 3: Journeyman

Journeyman listeners listen with their whole bodies, not just their ears. How many times have you been multitasking or heard someone talk about their ability to multitask? We hate to break it to you, but multitasking is a myth. Our brains cannot focus on more than one thing at a time. They are, however, fantastic at switching between tasks quickly. This switching quickly between tasks comes with a cost. It requires energy for the brain to switch between tasks. The energy expended switching between tasks lowers the brain's ability to execute both tasks at its maximum ability. Doing anything but listening negatively impacts your ability to listen. It also sends negative feedback to the person speaking. If you are busy doing something, anything, while your spouse is talking to you, you communicate that the task is at least as important as, if not more important than, what they are saying.[34]

When listening, position your body to be fully engaged in the conversation. Face the person speaking. Look them in the eye, or at least in their general direction. This doesn't mean stare them down. It means show with your face and body that you are open to what they are saying and that you are paying attention to them.

Put everything down. Don't have anything in your hands. Anything that you can fidget with or play with will distract you. Put those cell phones in your pocket on silent. If it doesn't distract you, it can distract the person talking. Either way it detracts from the conversation.

Level 5: Craftsman

A craftsman listener listens to the whole message of the speaker, no matter how long they take to make their point. Most people do not listen to everything they hear. They listen only long enough to comprehend the point they believe the speaker is making. From that point forward, the listener is usually thinking about their response to the point rather than what the speaker is actually saying.

To say this kind of listening is poor is too generous. It is selfish listening. It invalidates the person speaking and devalues the message they are sending. It places a higher importance on the response of the listener, rather than the message of the speaker. James instructs us to "be quick to listen, slow to speak, slow to anger" (James 1:19). Listening well is not just a product of our times; James noticed this in the first century as well.

When you listen simply to reply and be heard yourself, you present a

---

[34] This does not necessarily apply to every conversation. It is completely acceptable to cook, or clean, or work on hobbies while having casual conversation. Just be sure that the conversation is casual and not something that the speaker believes deserves a higher level of attention.

significant LIMFAC to yourself as the listener; you are unable to understand the message of the speaker. First, conversational speaking is not like public speaking. Conversations are rarely mapped out with an introduction, body, and conclusion. Conversations are extemporaneous. As the speaker speaks, they hear their words, take feedback cues from the listener, and alter their delivery to as clearly as possible communicate their message. This means that the first expression of the thought may be incomplete or inaccurate. Only by listening to the whole message will the listener be able to as fully as possible comprehend the intended message.

Second, listening to only respond rather than understand the speaker engages rather than mitigates the biases of the listener. Dietrich Bonhoeffer rightly noted that "There is a kind of listening with half an ear that presumes already to know what the other person has to say."[35] In every conversation you enter, you may correctly or incorrectly presume what the speaker is going to say; either way, you are not fully hearing the speaker. When you do not focus on the full expression of the message, you limit your understanding of the content to what you believe they are intending to say. You bring all of your history to bear on the topic with no attempt to overcome your history and preconceptions about the topic. In so doing, you decide what the message is supposed to be rather than what the message actually is. You may as well have the conversation with yourself because the actual thoughts and message of the speaker are overwhelmed by your presuppositions.

Jen has dealt with this many times while dealing with particularly brash opposing counsel. These are lawyers so wrapped up with their own egos that they fail to advocate for their own clients and resolve matters without a judge's involvement. There was a time when Jen met an opposing counsel in a courtroom hallway before the hearing. He thought that he could bully Jen and her client into an agreement based on the limited information that he had and lies that his client had told him. The other lawyer's client had been stealing money from her own mother and Jen and her client had the condemning documentation and other evidence to prove it. This lawyer could have mitigated the penalties that the court ultimately imposed on his client had he listened to Jen, taken the evidence against his client seriously, and made arrangements to put the money back. Oftentimes, when lawyers

---

[35] Bonhoeffer, *Life Together*, 52.

listen to each other regarding what their respective clients need and want, they can creatively come up with a solution that works for all parties.

To fully listen to the whole message of the speaker, discipline yourself not to think about anything but the words they are saying and how they are communicating their words. Listen carefully to the individual words, how they are put together in sentences and thoughts. Pay close attention to the tone and pitch of the speaker. Do they sound excited, sad, agitated, confused? Watch their body language. What does their body communicate about the message? Are they aggressive, defensive, or stressed? Use verbal cues to communicate that you are listening and that you care. Utterances while focusing on what is being said such as, "uh huh, really?, that's interesting," etc. when spoken by the listener to the speaker can encourage elaboration on the topic and also feelings of being understood. When you are unclear, ask clarifying questions like, "Do you mean ...?" or "Can you elaborate on that?"

Once the speaker is finished speaking, reflect back to them what you heard them say. Summarize what you understand the message to be. Ask if you have heard them correctly. Allow the speaker to clarify if you have not heard them correctly.

Most importantly, do not think about what you want to say until they are done speaking. This requires discipline. It requires focus. It is hard. Do not beat yourself up for being unable to do this perfectly. When you find your mind wandering, thinking about work or how you want to respond, force yourself to stop and single mindedly think about the words that the speaker is saying.

This type of listening also requires trust. One of the reasons people often spend time thinking about what they want to say while another is talking is because they are afraid they won't get a chance to make their point. Remember *Team Marriage*. Your spouse cares a great deal about what you want to say. They love you incredibly. The reason they are talking to you about this is because they care. Trust them. They will listen to you in the same way you are listening to them.

Level 9: Superintendent

A superintendent listener listens prepared to be changed by what they hear. Let's go back to the beginning of the book now. Marriage is a spiritual union. It is a process through which two individuals become one couple. The ultimate goal of marriage is for the two individuals in the couple to become more like Jesus. The goal is holiness. You cannot become more holy and not change. Change is a necessary component of any form of growth and development. As you listen to your spouse, listen with humility. Listen knowing that together you and your spouse are "working out your salvation with awe and reverence" (Philippians 2:12). No one on earth knows you better than your spouse. No person on earth loves you more than your spouse. Listening to them with humility and prepared to be changed by what you hear is the proper and holy response to the love they are expressing to you by having the conversation with you.

Conclusion

Listening is perhaps the best way to communicate love. Yet, most of us are not good listeners. Listening is a skill that everyone agrees is important. Most people, however, do not spend time developing their listening skills. In some cases, they are not aware of their lack of listening skills. In others, they do not know how to develop the skills. We propose four ways to help you develop your listening skills: (1) eliminate distractions, (2) listen with your whole body, (3) listen to the whole message, and (4) listen and be prepared to be changed.

Action step:

Discuss together the following questions:

- What do you think are your biggest distractions?
- What do you think your spouse's biggest distractions are?
- What can you do together to mitigate those distractions?
- How can you help each other listen with your whole bodies and focus on the whole message?

CHAPTER 12

INSIDE VOICE/OUTSIDE VOICE: PERSONALITY DIFFERENCES TO UNDERSTAND AND EMBRACE

We've all heard it, "opposites attract." Perhaps it's confirmation bias, but one thing we've seen over the years is that opposites tend to attract in one aspect. Introverts and extroverts are often attracted to each other. While this may not be a fundamental social law, we've experienced it often enough that we feel it deserves some discussion. It bears discussion because introverts and extroverts have fundamental differences that they often do not understand in each other. We were married seven years before we better understood the significance of the differences between us.

Defining Terms

Introversion and extroversion are often defined socially. Most people define extroverts as those who are energized by crowds and social interaction. Introverts are then defined as people who are energized by being alone. This social dimension of introversion and extroversion is one way to define the terms. It is the common definition and most people have already learned how to manage these differences. While the social definition of the terms is important, in this case we want to focus on an intellectual definition of the terms.

Less commonly discussed but equally important definitions of introversion and extroversion focus on how individuals process information. Introverts process information internally. They are most comfortable taking in information processing it quietly by themselves then talking about their conclusions. Extroverts prefer to process information externally. They like to talk things out. They think through a topic by talking about it.

Understanding this distinction has been very important for us. It has helped us navigate issues and conversations by helping us understand where the other is in processing things. We were married almost ten years before we learned this distinction and how it affects us and our communication.

In chapter 7 we mentioned that Jen is an extrovert and Bryon is an introvert. Jen thinks out loud and processes things verbally. Bryon processes things internally. He often stops talking in the middle of sentences because he's not sure what he wants to say. He pauses, thinking things through, then finishes the sentence.

This difference became very apparent after we moved from our first home together in Northville, Michigan to our current home in Ann Arbor, Michigan. As a family we experienced a lot of changes that year. Bryon resigned his position as chaplain of a Christian school to focus on new ministry endeavors. Our second child, Jonathan, was born. Plus we moved. That was a lot to process.

Jen talked a lot about things that were going on. She talked about her feelings, her concerns, her fears. She would bring up the same topic almost every day for a couple of weeks. To Bryon, this was an indication that something was weighing very heavily on Jen. For her to talk this much about one subject must mean it is particularly troubling to her. Bryon, the introvert, thinks about a topic about twice as much as he talks about it. To him it seemed that Jen must be constantly fixated on one topic to talk about it so much.

When Jen would start talking about a topic we had already discussed many times before, Bryon would go into problem solving mode. This issue, to him, was clearly a major issue that required action for resolution. He would get frustrated that Jen seemed to ignore his help and would rather keep her problem than resolve the issue. Jen would get equally frustrated with Bryon. She was just thinking through things and had not come to any conclusions. Bryon was getting emotionally amped up over issues that were not that important, simply things she was thinking through.

During this same time, Bryon attended some ministry training in California. Part of this training included understanding different aspects of a person's personality. During the training, Bryon and his colleagues learned about their own personalities and how those personalities interact with other personalities.

During this training, Bryon learned the difference between how introverts and extroverts process information. It was a huge "aha!" moment for him because in our marriage we were facing this exact issue. When Bryon starts talking about an issue, he has usually already thought it through pretty thoroughly. Usually, he has already come to a tentative conclusion and is now looking for feedback to see where his thinking was faulty or to refine his plan of action for better results. This is not true for Jen. When Jen starts talking about something that is important or of interest to her, that is often the moment she started thinking about it. She has spent little to no significant time processing the issue up to this point and has often come to no concrete conclusions.

Through this experience, Bryon learned that he needs to be more patient with Jen and a better listener. He needs to listen to her without making any judgments or conclusions. The better he listens, the better he is able to understand what Jen is thinking and be a useful sounding board.

Jen already knew that Bryon was quiet and thoughtful. She learned that she needs to be aware of this when she's thinking out loud. She can't presume that Bryon knows where she is in processing an issue. She has to let him know what she needs from him at a given moment. She knows now to tell Bryon if she is still in the early stages of processing things and not ready for concrete inputs. When she is ready for substantive feedback, she asks for it, helping Bryon know what role he needs to play in the conversation.

Bryon, on the other hand, has just about made his mind up when he starts talking about something. When we were dating, Bryon told Jen that he was thinking about getting a tattoo. To Jen, this meant he was merely considering the prospect and that it may have been a passing whimsical thought. She had no idea how much time he had spent thinking about the decision. Bryon showed up at her house the next day with a new tattoo.

Jen was shocked! Bryon said he was thinking about getting a tattoo, but really he had *decided* to get a tattoo. But these are differences that we've learned to navigate, so when Bryon starts talking about something, Jen knows that it's likely not just ideas or musings; it's more likely that an action will occur very soon.

Great Story, So What?

This chapter is more than simple stories about how we learned about and navigated a significant difference between the two of us in our marriage. We think this is a key issue in marriage that many couples struggle to navigate. Christian premarital counseling rarely addresses personality and the effects it has on marriage. We've been involved in premarital counseling for several years and the literature that we've used has never significantly addressed it; but we are certain to address personality differences with engaged couples.

There are examples throughout the Bible showing many differences between personalities of people, many of them family members. Just to name a few: Jacob & Esau; Leah & Rachel; Joseph & Judah; Moses & Aaron; and Peter & Thomas. The Apostle Peter gives husbands and wives advice on how to treat each other well by honoring their differences. In 1 Peter 3 he then advises all believers to "be harmonious, sympathetic, affectionate, compassionate, and humble" (3:8). Understanding and respecting differences isn't always intuitive or easy, but it's always worthwhile so that you can construct a healthy marriage while honoring God and each other.

When you consider how long we had been married plus the time we dated, it took us fourteen years to learn the full impact of personality differences and how to honor them. We truly think learning this sooner would have had a significant positive impact on our relationship. We hope that sharing this with you will challenge you to take the time to learn more about yourselves and how your personality differences affect your marriage.

It would take a whole book to discuss all the aspects of personality and how they affect marriage, and there are already a lot of very good resources out there. We recommend you take the time to do personality assessments.

Once you've completed the assessments share the results with each other. Take some time to learn both about yourself and your spouse. Discuss what you learn and how you will use it to improve your relationship.

There are many different personality assessments available. Our favorite is the Meyers-Briggs Type Indicator (MBTI). It is well researched and has stood the test of time. There are a lot of free resources available online. Simply search MBTI. Also, look into Enneagram and DISC. There is no judgment on which personalities are better or worse than others. As far as we're concerned, all personalities are great; they are just different. Knowing yourself and your spouse better gives you more tools to connect and resolve differences. And that's something to help you grow together and lead to a healthy marriage.

Action step:

Use a personality test or more as described above. This week, ask yourselves and then discuss:

- What are our known differences in personalities? Similarities?
- How do these balance us out well as a couple?
- What do we need to understand better about each other?
- Where do we need to extend more patience with each other?

CHAPTER 13

SERVING EACH OTHER

When Bryon officiates a wedding, he sits down with the couple at the first planning meeting and spends some time getting to know them and learns a little about the story of their relationship. A wedding is a very personal ceremony and Bryon works hard to make sure that the ceremony reflects the couple. After hearing their story, he starts going over the elements of the ceremony. With the information he gathered hearing the couple's story, he is able to help guide them to make the ceremony unique to them.

Many couples have no idea what elements they want in the ceremony. They just want to get married. Those wedding ceremonies are easy to plan. Bryon gives the couple a short list of choices for each element and helps the couple make the decisions.

Some couples have very specific visions of what their ceremonies should be like. Those are a little trickier. Not because the couple is difficult, rather because it is often hard for Bryon to translate what they are telling him into a cohesive ceremony.

The first wedding Bryon ever officiated was the second type. The couple had some very clear expectations of what they wanted in the ceremony. More importantly, however, they had some very clear expectations of what they did not want in the ceremony. Both people found the "love and obey" language for wives in the old vows offensive. In their vows and throughout the ceremony they wanted to emphasize that their marriage would be characterized by mutual service between the two of them.

The verse they chose for the theme of their ceremony was Ephesians 5:21-27:

Wives, submit to your husbands as to the Lord, because the husband is the head of the wife as also Christ is the head of the church—he himself being the savior of the body. But as the church submits to Christ, so also wives should submit to their husbands in everything. Husbands, love your wives just as Christ loved the church and gave himself for her to sanctify her by cleansing her with the washing of the water by the word, so that he may present the church to himself as glorious—not having a stain or wrinkle, or any such blemish, but holy and blameless.

Although it is vital to understanding marriage, we often get frustrated when we hear people talk about this passage because it is so widely misinterpreted. Misinterpretation has led to abuse in some marriages and animosity from people who do not understand the proper biblical vision of marriage. This misunderstanding comes from a misunderstanding of the social context of the family when Paul wrote this.

The family structure in the ancient world did not consist of a father, and a mother, with two and a half children as it does in the West today. A household when Paul wrote these words was a complex economy, with a head of household, yes, but also a wife who was probably more influential where the purse strings were concerned, a large extended family expanding in several directions, many children, servants, business associates, guests that were coming and going, staying longer and shorter periods of time, as well as slaves. That alone should tell you that Paul was dealing with a different world.

When reading Ephesians 5:21-27 in its larger context you will see that Paul wrote to this complex family structure and was calling all levels to mutual submission and love. He was calling them to recognize responsibilities. Paul did not wish to establish authority. Authority already existed in the culture. Paul was calling Christian families to something greater. He challenged all to achieve new and deeper levels of servanthood.

Regarding this servanthood it is particularly important to understand what Paul was saying about husbands, because he actually raises the stakes for men in marriage. Men have a greater responsibility of service and submission because men are to love their wives as Christ loves the church. Paul describes this love in Philippians 2:5-8:

> Let the same mind be in you that was in Christ Jesus, who, though he was in the form of God, did not regard equality with God as something to be exploited, but emptied himself, taking the form of a slave, being born in human likeness. And being found in human form, he humbled himself and became obedient to the point of death - even death on a cross.

That is the death which gives us salvation and makes us children of God.

Many think that Paul's letter to the Ephesians establishes hierarchical levels of authority determining who gives the orders. Paul is doing just the opposite. The hierarchical structure already existed. Everyone already knew who gave the orders. He took the structure that already existed and turned it upside down, insisting that we emulate Jesus in serving each other, and remembering that Jesus said whoever would be the greatest among us would actually be the greatest servant.

In the true biblical family all members will find their greatest joy in striving to be the greatest servant, sacrificing the most, taking the other's feelings into account, choosing what the other might wish to do, giving up cheerfully, without pointing attention to the fact, so that all may be built up in Christ's love. This is what the letter to the Ephesians is truly describing. This is what Christian marriage is truly about.

Yeah, But Why Is It So Hard?

We don't think this is new information to you. We know you are familiar with and even agree that marriage, when working right, is characterized by mutual service. We discussed this in Chapter 5: *Becoming One*. Our goal in this chapter is to help you apply what you already know to your marriage today. To do that, it's important to understand why it's so hard.

The problem can be summed up in one word: pride. The reason it is hard for us to consistently serve one another in love is pride. In *Mere Christianity* C. S. Lewis says:

> Well now we have come to the centre. According to Christian teachers, the essential vice, the utmost evil, is Pride. Unchastity, anger, greed, drunkenness, and all that, are mere fleabites in comparison: it was through Pride that the devil became the devil: Pride leads to every other vice: it is the complete anti-God state of mind.[36]

The original sin was pride:

> The serpent said to the woman, "Surely you will not die, for God knows that when you eat from it your eyes will open and you will be *like divine beings* who know good and evil."

> When the woman saw that the tree produced fruit that was good for food, was attractive to the eye, and was desirable for making one wise, she took some of its fruit and ate it. She also gave some of it to her husband who was with her, and he ate it (Genesis 3:4-6, emphasis added).

Other translations say "you will be like God" (ESV, NIV, NKJV, NLT). The original sin was in not being content: being human but wanting to be more. Pride in this sense is putting one's self at the center of their reality. It is a radical self-centeredness that affects all humanity. As C. S. Lewis said, "It is Pride which has been the chief cause of misery in every nation and every family since the world began. ... Pride is spiritual cancer: it eats up the very possibility of love, or contentment, or even common sense."[37]

This radical self-centeredness is the root of what Paul refers to as the

---

[36] C. S. Lewis, *Mere Christianity*, (London: Harper Collins, 1952), 131, Kindle Edition.
[37] Ibid. 134, 136

sinful nature (NLT), or the flesh (ESV, KJV, NET, NIV). When we think so highly of ourselves it is hard to serve because we think too much of ourselves and our needs to acknowledge and/or care about someone else's needs. When we do work to provide for another, our pride focuses on the effort we put into the service rather than the needs of the other person. Pride makes it difficult for us to think about another person at all unless it is in relation to ourselves.

In a *NY Times Magazine* review of the 2010 movie *Monogamy* by Dana Adam Shapiro, Adam Sternbergh described how Shapiro got the idea of the movie. Upon returning to his hometown, he was surprised by the number of his friends that were divorced. He started doing some anecdotal research as to the cause of breakup. The ultimate result was his movie.[38]

The interviews reprinted in Sternbergh's article all have a similar theme: self-centeredness. In each of the interviews, the interviewee describes their own self-centeredness. The natural response to self-centeredness is self-centeredness. Humans, thanks to the fall, are naturally self-centered. This cycle of self-centeredness ultimately led to divorce in the cases of those interviewed by Shapiro. The resulting movie takes a very dim view of marriage, questioning if a thriving, healthy marriage is really nothing more than a myth.

Shapiro came to his dim conclusion of marriage because he saw the result of sin in unredeemed humanity. In marriages that fall apart like the ones Shapiro researched, there is no mutual service. In his book *The Meaning of Marriage*, Pastor Tim Keller writes:

> The main barrier to the development of a servant heart in marriage is what we touched on in the first chapter— the radical self-centeredness of the sinful human heart. Self-centeredness is a havoc-wreaking problem in many marriages, and it is the ever-present enemy of every marriage. It is the cancer in the center of a marriage when it begins, and it has to be dealt with.[39]

---

[38] Adam Sternbergh, "A Brutally Candid Oral History of Breaking Up", *New York Times Magazine*, (March 11, 2011, https://www.nytimes.com/2011/03/13/magazine/mag-13Monogmy-t.html), accessed Jul 11, 2020.
[39] *The Meaning of Marriage*, 48-49.

The reason that consistent mutual service is so hard is because we are still in the process of overcoming sin. We are also still in the process of becoming more holy.

Holy Service

The purpose of marriage is to make us more holy. Becoming more holy means becoming more like Jesus. One of the key characteristics of Jesus' life was that he was humble. The gospel is about Jesus' humble sacrifice originating in his love of people and desire to save people from sin. The mission of all Christians is to become more like him.

You should have the same attitude toward one another that Christ Jesus had,

> who though he existed in the form of God
> did not regard equality with God
> as something to be grasped,
> but emptied himself
> by taking on the form of a slave,
> by looking like other men,
> and by sharing in human nature.
> He humbled himself,
> by becoming obedient to the point of death
> —even death on a cross! (Philippians 2:5-8)

If marriage is intended to make us more holy, then it is intended to make us more humble. As we serve each other, we learn to become more humble.

As we grow in holiness our self-centeredness decreases. We become less prideful. Holy people are humble people. Humility is acknowledging our place before God and responding to the world with his love accordingly.

To have a healthy marriage that leads you to be more humble and more holy is simple, but it is not easy. It requires effort. It requires concentrated focus. It is not, however, a focus on yourself. You can focus on yourself and modify your behavior, but that will not make you more humble or holy. When you focus on yourself and your behavior you are setting yourself up to be rewarded for the good things you've done. This is just another form of pride and C. S. Lewis argues it is particularly pernicious and devastating. A humble person "will not be thinking about humility: he will not be thinking about himself at all."[40]

To become more humble, therefore, means to think about yourself less. Marriage is the perfect context in which to practice and learn humility. You already love each other. You already want what is best for each other. You are already a team. The next step is to intentionally think about the wants and needs of your spouse. As you think about their wants and needs you will naturally think a little less about your own. You only have so much bandwidth.

As you are thinking more about those wants and needs, the next step is to think about how to meet those needs. Think about what you can do to serve your spouse. It would be useless for us to provide a list of examples here. Your marriage is different from ours. Your spouse has different wants and needs. You have to do the work of thinking about it and meeting those wants and needs.

We find that it is common to not know how to serve each other at a given moment. It isn't always obvious how best to serve in a given situation. In those times, when you don't know how to serve, simply ask your spouse. Ask what you can do to help in that moment.

When asking, however, ask "What can I do to help?" not "Can I help?" Especially in America, we are programmed to say "no" when someone asks "Can I help?" We do it without even thinking about it. It's a reflex response. When asked the open-ended question, "What can I do to help?" we are more likely to think about the situation. We are more likely to think of a way the person asking can help.

As hard as you work to consistently serve your spouse, you are still likely to make mistakes. You are going to be selfish and not serve when you should. There are times when your attempts to serve are going to backfire and make the situation more difficult. That's why marriage is such a great context in which to serve.

First, no matter what happened last time, there will always be another opportunity to serve. You will never exhaust your opportunities to serve in your marriage. If you were unsuccessful last time, try again, and again,

---

[40] Mere Christianity 127

and again, and again. Never give up. Serving like anything else is a skill: the more you do it the better you get at it.

Second, your spouse loves you. If you fail to serve in a time when you should, they will forgive you. If you screw things up when you try to serve, they will forgive you. The loving thing to do when you fail or make things worse is to apologize and seek forgiveness. You both are interested in what is best for each other. Your spouse will certainly forgive you. And forgiveness is a type of service to each other!

The Holiness of Receiving Service

Receiving service from each other can be just as difficult as serving each other. The reason is the same. Pride. Pride keeps us from humbling ourselves enough to receive help. We are conditioned to be independent. It starts in childhood. As soon as they can talk, almost every child says, "Let me do it!" Independence seems to be hardwired into our psyches. We think this comes straight from our sinful natures. The desire to be like God was the desire to be independent of him. We do not like to depend on anyone for anything.

Independence will kill your marriage. To have a healthy marriage that lasts a lifetime, you need to think about your spouse. You need to give them the opportunity to serve you. You can't do everything on your own. It is prideful to try to do everything without their involvement. It's easy to say that you're just trying to serve them and that you don't want to be a burden on them. In reality, that is your pride. You are trying to prove to someone, perhaps just yourself, that you do not need help. When you constantly refuse help you are thinking more about yourself than your spouse.

To overcome your pride in this area, allow your spouse to help. First when asked, "what can I do to help?" think about the question. Try to find something they can do to help. The experience of helping and being helped will strengthen the bond between you. Second, ask for help. There are things with which you need help. You cannot do everything on your own. When you need help, ask.

Express Appreciation

With everything that has been said above, it may seem like expressing appreciation is not important. The goal is holiness. The goal is humility. The goal is thinking of yourself less often. Isn't appreciation just feeding ego? For the prideful, yes. Arrogant, prideful people are constantly seeking affirmation and appreciation. That is, however, not true for those that are humble. Appreciation expressed to truly humble people is gratifying because it lets them know that the person offering gratitude truly appreciated the help. It reinforces that they were thinking about the other person.

We bake a lot of cookies in our house. We bake cookies at least once a week. One evening Jen put the cookies in the oven then went downstairs to the family room in the basement. Bryon was reading in the living room. When the timer went off, Bryon got up and pulled the cookies out of the oven. He knew that Jen was downstairs and it was easier for him to get the cookies than her. Jen heard the timer go off and Bryon moving around upstairs. She called up "Bryon, did you get the cookies out?" Bryon responded on the way back to his book, "Yes, I did." As he headed back to his book he heard Jen from the basement, "My hero!"

Jen was truly grateful that Bryon got the cookies out of the oven. It was something she could easily have done. She expected to do it. She was the one baking cookies. She would have had to stop what she was doing and come up the stairs to pull them out. Bryon knew she was downstairs and that it would be easier for him to get them. He had to put his book down, but it was worth it because he was making things a little easier for Jen. He was thinking more about Jen's convenience than his desire to keep reading.

Bryon felt good that Jen appreciated his action. He wasn't seeking affirmation or appreciation. He was trying to be helpful to Jen and express love to her by serving her. That simple event, an act of service and expression of appreciation strengthened the bond between us. A simple moment that lasted less than a minute made our marriage thrive a little bit more.

Conclusion

Mutual service is essential to a thriving marriage that will last a lifetime. It is the point that Paul made to families in the book of Ephesians and a consistent theme about relationships between believers throughout Scripture. Mutual service as an essential element to a healthy marriage is self-evident. It is, however, difficult. It is difficult because our pride gets in the way of our service. Yet, that is exactly the point. The purpose of marriage is to make us more holy. Holy people are humble people. Marriage provides us the perfect environment to become more humble as we focus on thinking about each other rather than just ourselves. When we focus on the wants and needs of each other, rather than our own needs, our marriages become healthier.

Action step:

This week, make a point to think more about your spouse. Think about their wants and needs and focus on serving them. When your spouse serves you this week, make a point to show your sincere appreciation.

- How can you think about your spouse's needs more this week?
- How can you serve your spouse this week?
- How can you express appreciation to your spouse for his/her service to you?

CHAPTER 14

LET'S TALK ABOUT SEX

Sex is an uncomfortable thing to talk about. It may be because of the puritanical roots of our culture. It may be because of the level of intimacy that comes with it. It may be because the church tends to ignore the topic relegating it to "just say no" style messages in youth groups and brief conversations in premarital counseling. Whatever the reason, sex is an uncomfortable topic.

While sex is an uncomfortable topic, it is a topic in which people are very interested. While doing a survey of Christian books about marriage, we were surprised to see how many books on the topic of sex were out there. Almost half of the books we looked at discussed sex in detail. There were even a few books written solely about sex in marriage. This indicated to us that sex was an important topic in marriage.

Sex and the Bible

There is a lot of bad information available regarding what the Bible says about sex. This is probably because of how the church tends to handle the topic. A majority of the messages about sex are "just say no" messages targeting teenagers. As people are waiting longer to get married the same messages get dusted off and repackaged for single adults.[41] Around 2010, it was popular for megachurches to try to bring some more balance with sermons for married couples about sex. Unfortunately, the attempt was perceived by many as nothing more than a gimmicky attempt to get more people to show up on Sunday mornings and the moment ended without making a significant impact on church culture at large. It is, therefore, probably best to start our conversation with a summary of the biblical message on sex.

It has been mentioned often but is important to repeat, sex in itself is not dirty or sinful in the context of marriage. Like many things, it may become sin when handled in an ungodly manner but sex is not inherently sinful. To refute any assertion to the contrary, Paul writes in 1 Corinthians 7 that sex should be enjoyed in the context of marriage:

> each man should have relations with his own wife and each woman with her own husband. A husband should give to his wife her sexual rights, and likewise a wife to her husband. ... Do not deprive each other, except by mutual agreement for a specified time, so that you may devote yourselves to prayer. 1 Corinthians 7:2b-3, 5a

God created sex when he created humanity. In Genesis 2:24 Adam and Eve were said to become "one flesh." As discussed earlier in this book, although this phrase means something richer and more expansive than sex, sex was definitely considered part of it. Sex is an aspect of becoming "one flesh" in marriage and has always been a part of the understanding.

The effects of sin on sex were immediately apparent. The comfortable intimacy shared by Adam and Eve was immediately broken. Before the fall they were "naked; but were not ashamed" (Genesis 2:25). As soon as they ate the fruit "they knew they were naked; so they sewed fig leaves together and made coverings for themselves"(Genesis 3:7b). The easy intimacy between them was broken. Sex, then, was intended from the beginning

---

[41] We firmly agree that God intends sex for marriage only. We are not opposed to the "just say no" messages about sex. It is a problem, however, when the only message the church presents about sex is "just say no" because it is unbalanced and does not present the whole message of Scripture on the topic.

to be a vehicle for intimacy and bonding between a husband and wife. The biblical Hebrew euphemism for sex supports this claim. In biblical Hebrew the author will refer to sex as "knowing" someone. The Hebrew euphemism "to know" is used ten times in the Old Testament to refer to sexual activity. We believe this is the purpose behind the prohibitions against adultery (Exodus 20:14; Leviticus 18:20) and incest (Leviticus 18:6-18).

Science supports this understanding of sex. There has been a lot of research about sex and oxytocin. There is too much to cite here, but a quick internet search will yield many scholarly articles on the subject. In short, sex causes the release of the hormone oxytocin. Oxytocin has been called the bonding hormone because it facilitates bonding between people. Humans are biologically conditioned to bond with a person with whom they have sex. One of the purposes of sex is to facilitate intimacy and bonding between a husband and wife.

The second biblical purpose for sex is obvious: procreation of children. The first reference to people having sex is a reference to Adam and Eve having children. There is some scholarly debate regarding the "be fruitful and multiply" statement in Genesis 1:28. It can be interpreted either as a command or a blessing. Either way, for our purposes we can see clearly that God created sex for procreation.

The third purpose of sex is pleasure. It is ok to like having sex. It is ok to want to have sex with your spouse. Puritanical misunderstandings of sex confused this issue for decades, perhaps centuries, in the church. The fact is, however, that God intended sex, in part, for pleasure.

One obvious proof of sex being intended for pleasure is that it is pleasurable. Stop and think about this for a moment. Sex does not need to be pleasurable. If sex was only intended for procreation, pleasure would be unnecessary. Especially early in human history when children were necessary for survival, people would have had sex whether it was pleasurable or not in order to have children. We contend that because humans are created for intimacy and the intimacy between husband and wife is an aspect of bearing the image of God, humans would have sex to bond without the physical pleasure included in the experience.

The church has taught at times (and in some communities still does teach) that sex for pleasure is sin. We find this argument counter to the witness of the Bible. First, while there is no evidence of sex before the Fall, sex existed before sin entered the world. The command/blessing, "be fruitful and multiply" predates the Fall. It is impossible to know if sex was pleasurable before the fall but there is no reason to believe it was not. The fact is, we don't know.

Second, pleasure in sex is not included in the description of the curse upon creation because of the Fall. The only connection to sex in the description of the curse is that women will experience pain in childbirth and a description of the breakdown of the intimacy between husband and wife, "You will want to control your husband, but he will dominate you" (Genesis 3:16b). Enjoying sex is not part of the curse nor is it sin.

Third, there are specific references to enjoying sex in the Bible within the context of marriage.

> May your fountain be blessed,
> and may you rejoice in your young wife -
> a loving doe, a graceful deer;
> may her breasts satisfy you at all times,
> may you be captivated by her love always. (Proverbs 5:18-19)

The word translated here as captivated describes the behavior of someone who is drunk. It describes the unsteadiness of someone walking when they are very drunk. "It signifies the ecstatic joy of a captivated lover. It may also mean 'to be always intoxicated with her love.'"[42] The Song of Solomon[43] is a very graphic, poetic celebration of sex in marriage. At times the Song of Solomon has been interpreted as describing the love of God for Israel or the love of Jesus for the church. The Bible has many metaphors describing God as a jilted husband and Israel as a promiscuous wife (Hosea) and Revelation describes the church as Christ's bride, so it is understandable how some might make this mistake with Song of Solomon as well. When reading Song of Solomon, however, it is hard to see it as an allegory describing the love of God for us due to its incredibly graphic

---

[42] Proverbs 5:19 translators note, Biblical Studies Press, (2005), *The NET Bible First Edition; Bible. English. NET Bible.; The NET Bible*. Biblical Studies Press.

[43] Also called the Song of Songs in some translations.

nature.[44] The entire book is full of poems celebrating the passionate, intimate, physical love between the protagonists. The Bible is very clear that sex depicted in marriage is intended for the mutual pleasure of the husband and wife.

The Place of Sex in Humanity

The proper place for sex is in the context of marriage. Throughout human history sex has been misunderstood and misused. This is clear from the frequent biblical prohibitions of sex outside of marriage. Popular culture in America promotes misunderstanding and misuse of sex.

Since Freud popularized his view of psychoanalysis and human sexuality in the early 20th century, we in western culture have largely adopted a false view of sex. "Freud said that when you look at people's behavior, their one purpose in life is to be happy and that 'sexual (genital) love . . . [is] the prototype of all happiness.'"[45] This, of course, has led to a complete disregard for the value of sexual purity before marriage. In modern western culture, sex between consenting adults is considered good in all situations.

Unfortunately, the popular view of sex that grew out of the Freudian perspective promoted an old pernicious myth about sex in marriage The myth was traced back to the beginning of western literature by Denis de Rougemont in his book *Love in the Western World*. In summary, the myth states that sex should be a wild, unabashed, passionate experience every time. Anything less, according to this view, is substandard sex. This has led couples to believe that sex should only occur when both people are in an extremely high state of physical and emotional arousal.

A perfect example of this can be found in Shapiro's interviews:

> We had settled into a routine where we only had sex once
> a week or so, maybe even less. There was no variety, and
> no real mental or emotional rewards. There was none of

---

[44] For a good study on Song of Solomon

[45] Armand Nicholi, *The Question of God: C.S. Lewis and Sigmund Freud Debate God, Love, Sex, and the Meaning of Life*, (New York: The Free Press, 2002), 126, Kindle Edition.

the urgency or tension that makes sex so great — that sense of wanting to impress or entice someone. I also got really precious about conditions being just right. I had this idea that if I had sex when I didn't really want to, I would start to associate sex with being a chore or a burden and start to hate it. So I turned down or discouraged advances if I wasn't already "in the mood," which in turn made him less likely to make advances.[46]

Urgency, tension, and the desire to impress or entice someone does not make sex great. It makes sex exhausting. It will be much harder for sex to bring two people together or even be enjoyable if you feel like you're constantly being graded on your effort. Timothy Keller responds to this perspective on sex:

One of the reasons we believe in our culture that sex should always and only be the result of great passion is that so many people today have learned how to have sex outside of marriage, and this is a very different experience than having sex inside it. Outside of marriage, sex is accompanied by a desire to impress or entice someone. It is something like the thrill of the hunt. When you are seeking to draw in someone you don't know, it injects risk, uncertainty, and pressure to the lovemaking that quickens the heartbeat and stirs the emotions. If "great sex" is defined in this way, then marriage— the "piece of paper"— will indeed stifle that particular kind of thrill. But this defines sexual sizzle in terms that would be impossible to maintain in any case. The fact is that "the thrill of the hunt" is not the only kind of thrill or passion available, nor is it the best. ... But sex in a marriage, done to give joy rather than to impress, can change your mood on the spot.[47]

[46] *A Brutally Candid Oral History*
[47] *The Meaning of Marriage*, 71, 72.

Sex is mutual giving of self to bond two people together and bring pleasure to each other. When two people consistently give of themselves to each other in mutual love then sex may not always be wildly urgent and tense, but it will be great sex; and furthermore better and more consistent sex than the alternative outside of marriage.

The Place of Sex in Your Marriage

Sex is an important part of marriage. It is so important in fact that Paul told the married couple in Corinth not to withhold sex from each other:

> A husband should give to his wife her sexual rights, and likewise a wife to her husband. It is not the wife who has the rights to her own body, but the husband. In the same way, it is not the husband who has the rights to his own body, but the wife. Do not deprive each other, except by mutual agreement for a specified time, so that you may devote yourselves to prayer. Then resume your relationship, so that Satan may not tempt you because of your lack of self-control (1 Corinthians 7:3-5).

Sex is a good, healthy part of marriage and you should be having sex.

Remember, however, the purpose of sex. Every sexual encounter should be an experience of mutual love and sacrifice. As with everything else we've discussed in this book, intent matters. When having sex, the goal is the joy and fulfillment of your spouse, not your own personal joy and fulfillment. As you both focus on serving each other in love you will both experience sexual fulfillment.

With that in mind, there are a couple of additional notes we would like to include in this section.

Note 1: It is ok to say no, sometimes. You are not required to respond affirmatively to every sexual advance. There will be times when you are too tired. There will be times when you won't be in the mood because of emotions you're feeling, or stress you're experiencing. Saying no to sex is not saying I do not love you. It is saying I cannot love you in that way right now.

If your sexual advances are rebuffed, it does not mean your partner does not love you. It means that something else is going on in their life that requires attention. In this moment it is your responsibility to respond in love to the situation. The response may be as simple as choosing to go to sleep. It may mean staying up all night talking through what is going on. Whatever it is, your job is to respond in love to the needs of your spouse.

Note 2: Orgasm is not the goal of sex. Orgasms are great and we hope that your sexual experiences are full of them. They are not, however, the priority. Sex is an opportunity for you to enjoy each other physically and strengthen the bond between you. Sex is about expressing love to each other. Orgasms are certainly a nice part of this but it is possible to accomplish all of the goals of sex without orgasm. Mutual pleasure together (and often orgasms) should be pursued even if orgasms are not attained every single time.

Let's be honest: typically this is more of a concern for women than men. There are many reasons that orgasm will not happen in a specific sexual encounter, whether by a man or woman. All men and women respond differently to stimulation. There are a lot of books out there about the physiology and mechanics of sex.[48] If you have concerns or questions we encourage you to do a little research and learn more. Be open with each other about your thoughts and concerns. If it is something that you find is a particular issue for you, don't be afraid to go to counseling.

The important point here is to acknowledge that it is ok if orgasm does not happen with every sexual encounter, despite your best mutual efforts. Sex is mutual sacrifice and love; it is not a performance. Pressure to orgasm may also make it more difficult. Anxiety will cause sex to be a negative rather than positive experience.

Sex is an important part of marriage, but it is not the most important part of marriage. It can, however, be an indicator to how things are going in the relationship.

> The adage in sex therapy is that when sexuality goes well,
> it is a positive, integral part of your relationship, but not
> a major component. Sexuality contributes 15–20% to

---

[48] We recommend *The Good Girl's Guide to Great Sex* by Sheila Wray Gregoire and *Intended for Pleasure* by Ed and Gaye Wheat

couple vitality and satisfaction. However, when sexuality is dysfunctional, conflictual, or avoided, it assumes an inordinately powerful role, draining your relationship of intimacy and vitality while threatening relational stability.[49]

In other words, sex is less important to your relationship when your relationship is going well. When your relationship is healthy, you will be having sex often enough that you do not feel it is missing and you will be happy with your sexual experiences together. When there are problems in your relationship, one or both of you will feel like you are not having sex enough. One or both of you will also probably not be enjoying sex when you do have it. That being said, having more sex will not solve the problems you are facing. Fixing the other issues in your relationship will improve your sex life.

Of course, a spouse's travel for work or illness will cause time for you as a couple to be unable to have sex together. Take that time apart to invest in each other in other areas of your marriage. Then resume sex togehter when you are both able to do so and you mutually agree.

We've been asked many times by many couples if there is a right amount of times to have sex in a week, a month, even a year. Well, there is. And here's the magic number: whatever each couple mutually agrees. Why? Because you are the co-creators and co-collaborators of your marriage, including sex. Want a thriving marriage? Openly discuss and mutually decide aspects of your sex life together. Don't try to live western culture's dream or some other couple's dream. Decide together what is best for you two as a couple and accept the God-given gift of sex.

Conclusion

Sex is an important part of your marriage relationship. It was designed by God to bond the two of you together, bring you pleasure together, and (of course) is the means by which we have children. It is not, however, the pinnacle of the human experience. The goal of humanity is not to

---

[49] Barry McCarthy, *Rekindling Desire*, (New York: Routledge, 2020), 8, Kindle Edition.

experience as much sexual gratification as possible but rather to love God and enjoy him forever.[50]

Sex is, however, an indicator to the health of your marriage. When your marriage is healthy, you and your partner will be happy with your sex life. You will enjoy it but not find it to be particularly important to your personal or mutual happiness. When your marriage is unhealthy, sex will become more important to you personally and as a couple. You will also find your sex life less satisfying.

Action step:

- With your spouse, discuss what your sex life is saying about your marriage.
  - o If your marriage is healthy now, discuss how you will address things when your marriage is less healthy.
  - o If your marriage is unhealthy, discuss what issue other than sex is troubling you in your marriage.

Final Note

There are times when couples are having problems sexually and they cannot resolve it on their own. Since sex is an important way God has chosen to bond married couples together it can be very troubling when issues cannot be resolved. If you find yourselves in this situation where your sex life is not bringing you closer together and you cannot find anything else in your relationship that is causing the problem, seek out the help of a professional counselor. Ask your pastor for resources or try an internet search for "Christian Marriage Counseling."

---

[50] *Westminster Shorter Catechism*

CHAPTER 15

WHAT DID YOU EXPECT?

Social exchange theory asserts that relationship satisfaction rises or falls as individuals compare the benefits and costs of the relationship with their expectations. Relationship satisfaction, then results when the cost/benefit assessment meets or exceeds relationship expectations. Conversely, relationship dissatisfaction results when relationship outcomes fail to meet expectations.[51] This sounds like a lot of pressure on a married couple! In this chapter, we will help you to identify and manage expectations of yourself and your spouse so that you understand each other's perspectives and continue to move towards having a thriving marriage.

Managing Expectations

A lot of a lawyer's job is managing expectations. Everyone in the case has expectations of how things ought to be. The client, opposing counsel, opposing party, and the judge or mediator, all have expectations. Some of these expectations are realistic. Some are not. No matter what, none of the parties to the case will have all of their expectations met exactly how they want nor will the case go according to any one person's plan or preference. A lawyer has to make sure that everyone, particularly their client, understands this reality and then help their client to moderate and manage their expectations.

---

[51] Jeffrey Dew, "Debt Change and Marital Satisfaction Change in Recently Married Couples", *Family Relations*, 57 (January 2008), 60–71.

Managing expectations isn't just something lawyers have to do. We all manage expectations. At work we manage the expectations of superiors, subordinates, customers, suppliers, and colleagues. We juggle hundreds of expectations, meeting the ones we can meet and communicating the reasonableness (or the unreasonableness) of those we can't meet.

The hardest expectations to manage, of course, are our own. We have expectations about everything in our lives. Since they are our expectations they are, to us, perfectly reasonable. One of the most difficult things for us to deal with is when our own expectations are unmet. This is particularly true when it comes to our marriages.

Where Expectations Come From

Growing up, Bryon's family never locked the door during the day when his parents were home. When they weren't in school, Bryon and his sister would go in and out of the house without any concerns. Their family felt perfectly safe without locking the doors. There was never any concern of someone walking in the house uninvited. This was probably, in large part, because they lived on military bases. Most of the time, they lived in places that were guarded by military police and required official government identification for entry.

Jen's experience was different. She grew up in the suburbs of Detroit. It was a very safe neighborhood but not locked down like military bases. Jen had unfettered access in and out the back door to her backyard, but the front door was always locked. It didn't matter who was home.

We, therefore, had very different expectations regarding locking doors when we got married and moved into our first home together. Bryon would walk in and out of the house without a concern about locking doors until evening came. Jen wanted the doors locked at all times no matter who was home or what the time was.

These different expectations created one of the first conflicts in our marriage. Whether the doors were locked or not was not important to Bryon but it was very important to Jen. She did not feel safe not knowing that the doors were locked. By leaving the doors unlocked, Bryon made Jen feel unsafe and communicated a lack of love by his ambivalence. He didn't, however, realize that this was an important issue to Jen. Jen had to explain to him her concerns and how the unlocked doors made her feel. Once Bryon realized the importance Jen placed on locking the doors, he changed his behavior and began keeping the doors locked. It took some time for him to change his habits but now the doors are always locked.

We all have expectations about marriage and life together. These expectations come from many sources. Some, like the ones we described above, come from your family of origin. Others come from our friends and their successes and failures in their own relationships. Still more come from the marriages we see around us, both the real ones and the fake ones on television and in the movies. The sources of expectations are endless and they all affect our expectations in one way or another.

Unmet and Unshared Expectations

The tricky thing about expectations is that we often don't even know they're there until they go unmet. They're kind of like your big toe. They're important to life. We can't function without them. Imagine if you had to think every time you sat in a chair whether chairs were meant for sitting or that this particular chair would support your weight. What a waste of brainpower! So, we have expectations that things will work as they're supposed to and don't think about them until they don't. Kind of like we don't think about our big toe until someone steps on it. Then it hurts and it's the only thing we can think about. Similarly, we don't think about our expectations until they go unmet. Then it seems that the unmet expectation is the only thing we can think about. A significant source of conflict in marriage is unmet expectations.

You see, expectations do not lead to conflict in marriage. *Unmet* expectations can lead to conflict. Let's take a look at the example from our marriage we discussed earlier in this chapter. Jen expected Bryon to lock the door every time he passed through it. Bryon did not lock the door every time. When Jen found the door unlocked there was a gap between what she expected and reality. This gap made her uncomfortable. In this case, it made her feel unsafe. Since Bryon was not locking the door and thereby was making Jen feel unsafe, Jen felt that Bryon did not care about their safety. These feelings led Jen to feel negatively toward Bryon. She started feeling like they were not on the same team.

This process is true of all unmet expectations in marriage. One spouse has an expectation. The other spouse does not meet the expectation. The unmet expectation causes negative feelings in the spouse that had the expectation. That spouse then feels negatively towards the other because they did not meet the expectation. The first spouse will do one of three things with their feelings:

- Dismiss them and decide that it is okay that the expectation is not met.
- Do nothing about them, allowing them to fester and building negative feelings even worse than before about their spouse and the unmet expectation.
- Address the feelings and the unmet expectation with their spouse.

And let's be honest, we've all done all three at different points in time.

The other issue regarding expectations is unshared expectations. When dating and preparing for marriage, couples often find they have many shared expectations. These shared expectations draw them closer to each other. Yet every couple has unshared expectations. No two people ever got married having the exact same expectations of marriage. As we saw above, there are many sources of expectations in marriage. No two people have the exact same experiences in life. This is certainly true of people getting married. They come from different families. They have different experiences with peers and their families growing up. They respond differently to representations of marriage in the culture around them. All of these differences lead to unshared expectations.

Unshared expectations become exposed in marriage. Often they are exposed as unmet expectations. The other common place unshared expectations are exposed is discussing goals and plans. An example of this in our marriage is Santa Claus. Both of our families held to the tradition of Santa Claus. When we were children, both of us received Christmas presents from Santa. Since both of us are eldest children we both became aware of the truth of Santa before our younger siblings. In Bryons' family, Santa was a fun game to play and he was asked to not ruin it for his little sister. Together the family played the game for a long time. Both Bryon and his sister continued to get presents from Santa long after they had learned the true story of the character. Jen's family took a more definitive stance about Santa. Her parents insisted on the existence of Santa and would not allow Jen to deviate from it. They refused to allow anything to break the illusion for Jen's younger sister. They would not discuss Santa with Jen but only insisted on his reality.

When our first child was born, we had to decide how we would handle Santa Claus. For Bryon it was a fun tradition and game that he wanted to continue. For Jen it was a lie told to children and perpetuated by adults. She absolutely refused to lie about this to our children because she didn't want them to question our integrity. In particular, she was afraid that Santa would get connected with God because of Christmas. She did not want her children wondering if we lied to them about God since we lied to them about Santa. Ultimately, we chose to compromise. With our children, we neither confirmed nor denied the existence of the individual known as Santa Claus. We allowed the children to participate in the tradition, we even got annual family pictures with Santa at the mall. Santa, however, never gave the children Christmas presents. The only time they noticed that Santa never gave them presents was when they were old enough to know the true story of Saint Nicklaus; until then they enjoyed the magic of the tradition. When they no longer believed that an old fat guy in a red suit committed millions of "breaking and enterings" on Christmas Eve, we asked them to be respectful of other families and not spoil the fun for them.

In that case, our unshared expectations were revealed when planning how to deal with a parenting issue. Unshared expectations are also revealed when discussing goals. As you discuss financial goals, retirement goals, career goals, family goals, or any other goals, there will be times when unshared expectations are revealed. The general response to unshared expectations is different from the response to unmet expectations.

Usually couples are surprised when unshared expectations are revealed. It never occurred to them that the expectation was unshared. In some cases the expectations are not connected to core values or beliefs. The response is often, "I never knew you thought like that." This might be a response to your taste in a certain type of music or genre of movie. In these cases the unshared expectations become interesting conversations. Other times unshared expectations are connected to core values or beliefs. That response is often, "I can't believe you think like that." This might be how to spend the holidays and what side of the family to visit and when the visits will occur. In these cases, the revelation of unshared expectations is much more intense. There are three ways to respond to unshared expectations:

- Choose to follow your partner's expectations.
- Find a way to compromise.
- Insist that together you follow your expectations.

As with unmet expectations, we all have followed all three responses to unshared expectations.

Unvoiced Expectations

Unmet and unshared expectations are a struggle in every marriage. Every couple must deal with them. Unvoiced expectations, equally unavoidable, are, however, an even bigger cause of struggles in marriage. These are the expectations that you have that are never spoken aloud, yet still carry weight for you personally and you might not even be aware of them!

Some unvoiced expectations exist because you feel like they are self-evident. The expectation is so obvious and normal to you that you presume they are universal. They are often the result of patterns and habits with which you grew up. They are norms that, as far as you're concerned, apply to everyone and don't require communication. Everyone in every family does this all the time. They are deeply ingrained in you. They are such a part of you that you are probably even unaware they are there, until they go unmet.

Other unvoiced expectations are expectations on topics that are taboo. Everyone has topics about which they are uncomfortable talking. Some of these topics are things about which you are just squeamish. Others are topics about which you do not feel safe discussing. Sex is at the top of this list for most people in American culture. Because of the nature and intimacy of sex, we do not often learn how to have healthy conversations about sex when we are young. We, therefore, have trouble talking about it in marriage. In-laws are another such topic. Relationships with in-laws are tricky. Relationships with parents have a significant impact on all of us. The feelings we have for our families of origin run deep. This can make it incredibly difficult to talk about expectations we have for our in-laws, our in-laws have for us, or we have for our spouse regarding in-laws on both sides. For you maybe there are other topics that make you feel uncomfortable to discuss. We all have different expectations that are difficult to discuss.

Here's the thing about unvoiced expectations: first, they are still expectations. It still hurts when they go unmet. In fact, it often hurts more. The expectations that seem, to you, to be universal are connected to deep seated values or beliefs. When these expectations are unmet it challenges your fundamental views of yourself, your spouse, and your marriage. In both cases, expectations that seem universal and taboo are hard to discuss with your spouse. The difficulty in talking about these expectations makes it harder to address the feelings of hurt and anger. These feelings, left unaddressed, can then fester and cause further issues in your relationship.

Second, these expectations are unvoiced. No matter how close the two of you are, you cannot read each other's minds. I know it can feel that way sometimes, but it isn't true. Unvoiced expectations will often be unmet because they are unknown. The things you don't talk about because you don't think you need to, or because you don't want to, are things that will never be addressed. It is a perfectly toxic recipe for inevitable conflict.

Dealing With Un-Expectations

We believe that every conflict in marriage starts with one of these "un-expectations." No matter the topic, the conflict arose because of an un-expectation. There was an unmet expectation that brought about hard feelings. An unshared expectation caused a conflict about the future of your relationship. An unvoiced expectation was either unmet or revealed as unshared that led to frustration with each other. Think back to your last conflict. What un-expectation triggered the conflict? In the next several chapters we will discuss some common un-expectations couples face and how to address them. For the rest of this chapter we will discuss an approach to deal with un-expectations in general.

The first step in dealing with un-expectations, no matter what the expectation is, is to acknowledge the expectation. This requires self-awareness. You have to be self-aware enough to know what emotions that you're feeling in a given moment. You have to understand yourself and your reactions. When you notice yourself getting upset or angry, or you start feeling anxiety; when this happens, you must stop and acknowledge the feeling.

Once you acknowledge the feeling, identify *what* triggered the feeling. What is the cause of the emotion? Are you responding to something that your spouse just did or said? Was there something left undone? What happened just before or as the feelings started? That is the triggering event.

Now that you have identified the triggering event, it is time to identify the expectation. What did you expect to happen? If things had gone the way you wanted, what would have happened? Name the expectation. Say to yourself, "I expected…". For instance, I expected my husband to ensure all the doors are locked. I expected my wife to agree with me regarding firearms in the home. Be as specific as you can here. It is important to know what you expected. You cannot resolve any issues if you cannot identify what the issues are. We have had many conversations that went nowhere because one or both of us could not identify the issue. We were simply responding emotionally without identifying why we felt that way. The only way to deal with un-expectations, is to know what they are.

Unreasonable Expectations

Perhaps the trickiest part of dealing with un-expectations comes after you name the expectation. Now that you know what the expectation is, ask yourself, "Is this expectation reasonable?" We bring countless expectations into our marriages. Not all of these expectations are reasonable. Some expectations are unreasonable because of logistics. It is not reasonable to expect that your spouse will join you for trivia night every Thursday if they work a swing shift or the night shift. Some expectations are unreasonable because of temperament. It is not reasonable to expect an extroverted artist to want to stay home every night and play chess with you. Some expectations are unreasonable because of ability. It is not reasonable to expect the person that barely passed college math to help the children with AP calculus. Some expectations are unreasonable objectively. It is not reasonable to expect your spouse to want to have sex everytime you want. Some expectations are unreasonable because your spouse is human. It is not reasonable to expect your spouse to meet the needs that only God can meet. There are many expectations that are unreasonable. You have to be ready to admit that to yourself.

You must be willing to let go of expectations that are simply unreasonable. You are only hurting yourself and your marriage if you hold on to these expectations. You must make the conscious choice to stop expecting the expectations that are unreasonable. While that is easy to say, it can be very hard to do. Some expectations, although they are clearly unreasonable, are rooted deep inside us. These expectations often come from our families of origin. Do not be afraid to admit when you struggle with letting go of an unrealistic expectation. If you find that you are unable to let go of unrealistic expectations, it is time to see a licensed counselor. A counselor or therapist has the tools to help you uncover the source of unrealistic expectations and will help you learn to let go of them or manage them in a healthy way. You and your marriage will both be healthier.

Reasonable Expectations

While some expectations are unreasonable and must be let go, many expectations are completely reasonable. Just because an expectation is reasonable does not necessarily mean the expectation should be addressed. Before addressing an un-expectation with your spouse, determine how important the expectation really is. A commander for whom Bryon works will often ask, "Is the juice worth the squeeze?" This is a great metaphor. To get juice from a fruit, you have to squeeze the fruit. Oftentimes, it takes a lot of squeezing of a lot of fruit to get enough juice to drink. Before deciding to squeeze the fruit you have to decide how important it is to get the juice and how much juice you will get. Is the result worth the effort?

Some expectations are simply not worth addressing. Speaking of squeeze, Jen is a "squeeze the toothpaste from the middle" person. Bryon squeezes the toothpaste from the bottom. When we got married Bryon would see the toothpaste squeezed "incorrectly". This was an unmet, unshared, and unvoiced expectation. Thinking it through, however, Bryon did not find the expectation particularly important. For nearly 17 years at the time of writing this paragraph, Bryon has spent an extra fraction of a second squeezing all the toothpaste to the top of the tube every time he brushes his teeth with no adverse effects to his oral health or the health of our marriage.

Many expectations fall into the category of not important. For those expectations, like the unreasonable expectations, let them go. How do you know how important the expectation is? Simple: ask yourself how strong is your reaction? If it is something you notice as different from what you would normally do but there is no emotional response, it is not that important.

Only you can decide the importance of addressing an un-expectation. It is important to remember, however, that every conversation has an impact on the health of your marriage. Every conversation communicates how you love each other. Addressing important un-expectations will ultimately improve the health of your marriage and increase the love between you. You love each other very much and do not want to create an uncomfortable, unfulfilling, unloving environment. You both want a thriving marriage. Nitpicking and nagging, however, decreases the health of your relationship and the love between you. It creates an environment that feels performance-based not love-based. It will make you both feel like you are not on the same team. If the un-expectation is unimportant, then leave it unaddressed. If it is important, then address it.

Conclusion

Expectations are a reality of life. Not only are they a reality, they are necessary. It would be impossible to function in life without expectations. We expect the sun to come up tomorrow. We expect water to be wet. We expect our spouses to be there when we wake up in the morning. We need expectations.

Expectations, however, are the cause of many struggles that we face in marriage. The conflicts and frustrations that we experience in marriage all come from unmet, unshared, or unvoiced expectations. These un-expectations must be managed if we are to build thriving marriages that will last a lifetime.

Action step:

This week, take some time to think about a recent time where you faced an un-expectation. Write down the events that happened in the moment and the feelings you experienced.

- What was the un-expectation?
- How did you handle it?
- After reading this chapter, reflect and determine whether you handled it well.
  - o   If so, why?
  - o   If not, what would you do differently now?
- What do you hope to learn about managing un-expectations in the rest of this book?
- Share this with your spouse and talk about how you can help each other manage un-expectations.

CHAPTER 16

MONEY, MONEY, MONEY

Money is consistently cited as a reason for conflict in marriage. It typically is listed in the top ten reasons for divorce. Money is second only to infidelity as the cause of a marriage ending.

Money has a very significant place in contemporary American culture. It influences every area of our lives. The moment we are able to communicate our wants as children, we start becoming aware of money. Our parents start communicating their values regarding money in how they handle our desire for toys, trips, or fast food kiddie meals. Commercials tell us we can get that cool new toy for $19.99 plus shipping and handling (not available in Hawaii or Alaska). As we get older, we start looking for ways to get our own money so we can be free to spend it (or save it!) the way we want instead of relying on our parents. The longer we work and the more money we earn, the more we desire for more money to be free to do and to get all the things we want.

As we enter adulthood, we learn that money governs not merely wants, but needs. We need money to provide shelter for ourselves. We need money to provide for clothes for ourselves. We need money to provide for our food.

Money even determines the level of connectedness we have with people. It takes money to go out to coffee with friends. It takes money to be involved in social activities. Even game night requires money because someone had to buy the game. Our socio-economic status determines the relationships that we will form. Money determines that status.

Sadly, this is even true for our church community. Our church community will often be in a certain proximity to where we live. Money determines where we live and therefore the radius to which we can reach for a church community.

Money is ubiquitous. It is impossible to escape the influence of money. It's not surprising then that it has such a large impact on our marriages.

Negative experiences of money have a disproportionate impact on our marital health. Research has shown that conflicts around money last longer than other conflicts and are more likely to recur. Couples also indicated that conflicts about money were of greater importance in their marriage than other conflicts.[52]

Money, however, is rarely the cause of marital conflict. Conflicts about money are usually symptoms of deeper un-expectations in the marriage. In a study about the effects of paying off debt on marital happiness, it was noted that it wasn't only the debt that affected marital happiness. It was how paying off debt impacted other aspects of marriage. The impact of the debt on time together and perceptions of financial unfairness were significant.[53] Money wasn't the core problem. It was the stress of the debt. It was the obligations on time and energy that were created by the need to make the money to pay off the debt.

This book does not delve into Biblical money management. There are a lot of books already written on that topic. We would like to highlight one aspect of biblical money management here. Later in this chapter, we will talk about money being a tool. It is important to remember that the tool, money, was given to you by God for his purposes. As you read this chapter and consider how you will handle money as a couple, remember that God does have expectations as to how you will use the money he has given you to manage.

---

[52] Lauren M. Papp, E. Mark Cummings, and Marcie C. Goeke-Moray, "For Richer, For Poorer: Money as a Topic of Marital Conflict in the Home", *Family Relations* vol. 58 #1, https://onlinelibrary.wiley.com/doi/full/10.1111/j.1741-3729.2008.00537.x, accessed Nov 6, 2019

[53] Debt Change and Marital Satisfaction Change in Recently Married Couples, 60–71.

Money's Place in Marriage

If money is only the symptom and not the issue, then why do so many couples cite money as a significant cause for divorce? We think it's because money is an easy scapegoat. It is easy to say that he/she spends too much money. It is easy to say he/she is stingy with money. It is easy to say he/she works too much because they value money too much. It is easy to say he/she doesn't contribute enough money to the household. It is hard to address the feelings underneath. It is hard to examine the expectations that are impacted by money. It is hard to address selfishness, insecurity, jealousy, and all the emotions that are triggered by un-expectations around money.

Ask yourself this question: "What does money really mean to you?"

We were involved in some pre-marital coaching for a couple. The woman was happy that her fiance had gotten a raise and new position. He would now be making about the same as she was making, but she was upset about the increased business travel that came with his raise and new position. She acknowledged her dual feelings of pleasure and displeasure. She also said that her experience growing up with her ambitious mother and no contributions from her father made her want to succeed in her career. She wanted the stability of higher earnings so she would not need to rely on a husband. At the same time she wanted her husband to be making at least as much as her so they would be contributing equally financially to the marriage (unlike her father, who didn't contribute). Jen turned to the couple and asked, "So what does money *really* mean to you?"

Money means different things to different people. For some, money means security. For others, money means freedom. Still others see money as status. What about you? What does money *really* mean to you?

Look at that list you just read. Can money really deliver on its promise of security or freedom or status? No, not really. It can give the illusion of such things but it cannot promise such things. The value of money is not in having it; rather, the value of money is in how it is used. And that use is in the spending, investing, saving, giving, or whatever is done with it. Therein lies the fatal flaw in trusting money. Once the money is spent, it is gone. Money is not a naturally renewable resource, but often you can work to earn more. Unless it's by inheritance or a gift, money will not come to you without your effort.

To prevent or overcome conflict around money, the first step is to understand what money really is. Money is not the source of anything.[54] This is true in life and marriage. Money is not the source of happiness, freedom, or success. "Whoever trusts in his riches will fall, but the righteous will flourish like a green leaf" (Proverbs 11:28).

Money is not the source of anything; rather it is a resource. The Merriam-Webster Dictionary defines resource as:

a: a source of supply or support : an available means —usually used in plural

b: a natural source of wealth or revenue —often used in plural

c: a natural feature or phenomenon that enhances the quality of human life

d: computable wealth —usually used in plural

e: a source of information or expertise

The thing we want you to notice about this definition is that the value of a resource is not in having the resource but in what it can do. The value in the resource is what the resource permits you to do with it. This is true with money in your marriage. Money is a resource that helps you to meet your needs and fulfill your goals and dreams.

Read that again: money is a resource that helps you meet your needs and fulfill your goals and dreams. The main goal or dream, of course, should be to please God with how you use the resource he has entrusted to you. Money is a tool. Nothing more. Nothing less. Just like a hammer or a screwdriver, money provides the capability to accomplish a goal or task. It is a means to an end, never an end in and of itself.

So what are your goals and dreams? Are they aligned with God, Scripture, and his will for you? Is your perspective on money and how to use it aligned with God's values and principles? Do your conflicts have God in mind when it comes to money management or are you just focusing on how you would like money in your marriage to be used?

---

[54] Nope - money isn't the source of all evil. That's a typical misquote of the Bible. Here's what Paul actually wrote, "For the love of money is a root of all kinds of evil. Some people, eager for money, have wandered from the faith and pierced themselves with many griefs" 1 Timothy 6:10. Be careful about your view of money!

All marriages will experience conflicts regarding money management. The important thing is how you resolve the conflicts. The first step to resolving conflicts generated by money is understanding money's place in your marriage. Money is a marital resource. It is a tool you use to fulfill needs and achieve goals. Conflicts generated by money are not about money and not caused by money. Conflicts generated by money are caused by (you guessed it!) un-expectations regarding the use of money.

For many of you, this will require you to rethink how you approach money. The goal of money is not simply the accumulation of money. Having money will not give you peace, security, or happiness. The value of money is the use of money to meet your needs and goals.

This does not mean that money should be spent without thought. Meeting your needs and goals requires that you have money. Meeting many of your needs and goals requires that you save money. There are goals that you have today that cost more than the money you currently have. To meet those goals requires that you earn and save money. Remember, however, the end is not just having money in the bank, making gifts to charities, or accumulation of stuff and experiences. Following Biblical principles and having manageable and realistic goals for money to meet your needs and goals, whether buying a house, saving for retirement, making gifts to charities, or having emergency savings will help you act as a team and grow to act as one in your money management.

Not only is it important to remember that money is a tool and not an end in itself, it is important to remember that money is a marital tool. When you're married, there is no such thing as "his money" and "her money" there is only "our money". You've likely figured out that Jen earns more money than Bryon because lawyers tend to make more than pastors or military members. We've both continually cheered each other on as we achieve professional goals. Bryon is the first to celebrate Jen's practice growing and career awards that she received. Similarly, Jen is the first to be thrilled about Bryon's promotions and the first to stand up during a standing ovation when Bryon receives an award. Bryon doing better is better for Bryon, Jen, and our marriage; similarly, Jen doing better is better for Jen, Bryon, and our marriage. We've always talked about our career goals and pursued them together. Could we be making more money right now? Probably. But would the extra work and more hectic lifestyle be worth it to us? No way! That's why we've worked together and agreed to pursue the goals in our careers that we have pursued.

Unfortunately, marriages break up over money. Time and time again, Jen sees divorcing couples who are doing everything to hurt each other and come out financially on top. There was a professional woman who was a higher wage earner than her husband and the husband treated his wife like a free ride financially and did little to help around the house or with their son. After no resolution and a build up of resentment over years, the couple divorced. The major argument in the divorce case was over child custody; the husband wanted 50/50 custody, not because he wanted more time with the child but because he wanted higher child support payments. There was a lot of arguing, time invested, and attorney fees spent over this issue. In the end, the wife ended up agreeing to pay more money in spousal support to the husband in exchange for having more time with their son.

Take a moment to pause and think about what happened in that situation. The wife practically bought more time with her son. The husband sold time with his son. Their respective values were apparent by their actions over the course of the divorce. Don't be that couple. You both can do better!

Once you understand that money is a resource - a tool - you are well on your way to overcoming and preventing conflicts around money in your marriage. When you see money correctly, you will see that it isn't actually the money or lack of money that causes the conflicts. The cause of conflicts related to money in marriage is not money, it is how money is used. The cause of conflict around money is un-expectations.

Do you have thoughts about who should be managing the money in your marriage or deciding how it should be used? We talk about roles in your marriage in the next chapter, but wanted to make a note here, since this likely crossed your mind. Who should be managing the money in your household? The one who does it the best and has the availability to do it. It's important to keep the other spouse in the loop about what is happening, especially in the event that the money manager dies or is unable to act in the role. In the event of a tragedy like this, you set your spouse up to succeed if he or she knows the account passwords and how and when bills are paid.

What about decisions about purchases? We believe that you should have a discussion about lifestyle choices, come to agreements, and work towards these goals together. Don't overspend on a lot of little things and then not have the money for goals; at the same time, carve out a budget for things that you enjoy. Our daughter was introduced to Starbucks while volunteering at the zoo. She would buy (or have us buy) Starbucks for her daily if she could. We've told her that she can have Starbucks no more than once a week and twice a month is preferred. This gets her what she wants, but it does not become unmanageable or get in the way of other goals.

Here's another thing: it doesn't matter which spouse earns more money. You both have equal voices with how it's used. Don't think for a minute that the higher wage earner should dictate what happens with the income. Without the other spouse, especially if you have children, the higher wage earner would not be able to earn and put in the hours. Marriages do not thrive, if the higher wage earner would dare to lord the earnings over the other. God allowed the marriage, the income, and the means of the income. How will you then honor God in that? If there are difficult decisions to make about finances, pray for the Lord's wisdom and will and then discuss with each other. If you come to an impasse, discuss with trusted friends and advisors. If bringing people outside the marriage into the conversation, make sure you agree on the limitations of their involvement. You do not want to create an environment where advisors are weaponized to try to win an argument.

Money and Un-Expectations

In the previous section we explained that money is not the source of anything in life. It is a tool necessary to meet the needs and goals you have in your marriage. Conflict related to money comes from un-expectations about how money is used.

Sally and John have been married for five years. Both have good jobs that they enjoy and together they make a good living. Their only child, David, is just over a year old. Sally and John are talking about having a second child but want to wait until David is out of diapers. They currently live in a two-bedroom bungalow in a pleasant neighborhood that they bought about three years ago. Until recently, they would have said they had very little conflict in their marriage. Many of the common disagreements that couples have early in marriage were addressed in their premarital counseling. They took the lessons to heart and resolved most of the issues before they became significant. Lately, however, they find themselves fighting a lot about money.

Sally dreams of a bigger house a little farther out of town with a nice yard for David and his future sibling to play in that is in walking distance to one of the better elementary schools in town. She's regularly checking house prices in her ideal neighborhood. She sees that they will have to commit to a savings plan to save enough for a down payment on a house. She's crunched the numbers. If they commit to eating out less and go on less expensive vacations they'll have enough money saved in about four years, just in time for David to start kindergarten.

John loves to travel and have new experiences. He agrees that they will need a bigger house when they have their next baby but doesn't see the need to start saving now. As they stay in their current home they will build equity that plus a more moderate saving plan will give them enough of a down payment for a new house when they are ready to move. In the meantime, he wants to use some money to travel while David is still young and they are not restricted by his school schedule.

As you can see, Sally and John's disagreements aren't really about money but rather how the money is spent. Making more money would not solve their problem; Sally might want an even bigger home in another community and John might want to take longer and more exotic vacations. They would still have the same argument; it would simply be about allocating different amounts of money. The issues they need to resolve are what kind of lifestyle do they want now and in the future. They have un-shared expectations that they need to resolve. Sally and John's conflict around money stemmed from money as a tool to meet goals.

We stated above that more money would not resolve Sally and John's conflict. Money, however, is not only a tool necessary to meet goals. It is also a tool to meet needs. Conflict can also occur when facing un-expectations around needs. These occur when a couple disagrees about the priority of needs or defining the difference between needs and wants. For instance one may feel that a reliable vehicle is a need to get back and forth to work while the other may believe that walking and public transportation are viable options. Un-expectations around needs also occur when couples disagree about who should work and how much. One spouse may think that the ideal is for only one spouse to work so the other can take care of the home and children while the other thinks that a dual-income family is the only way to meet needs. One spouse may believe that more overtime is necessary to meet needs while the other may think cutting expenses in wants is a better option.

Cutting expenses in wants to cover the cost of needs is almost always a good option. The reality is, when needs go unmet, the best option may be for you as a couple to increase your income. Money cannot buy happiness but lack of the money that you need will make you miserable. Are you able to make adjustments to your budget to spend less? Perhaps if one of you is not working, it is time to get a job. Perhaps pursuing more overtime or a second job is necessary. The solution will always be in addressing the un-expectation you are facing and developing a plan to resolve it.

Conclusion

Money is implicated as one of the leading causes of conflict in marriage and divorce. While money is integral to life today, it is not money that causes conflict. Money is merely a tool necessary to meet needs and goals in life. Blaming money for conflict in marriage is like blaming the hammer for the wall being crooked. The hammer did not cause the wall to be crooked; it was the error by the person who used the hammer and built the wall. Similarly, money does not cause conflict in marriage. The problem was caused by its use. The cause of conflict relating to money in marriage is often un-expectations regarding how money should be used in marriage.

Action step:

Think about a conflict you have had about money in your marriage.

- What was the root issue?
- What did you want to use money for?
- What did your spouse want to use the money for?
- What was the un-expecation you faced?

- Has the conflict been resolved?
  - o If so, how did you resolve the conflict?
  - o If not, take some time today to discuss your un-expectations with your spouse. Don't expect to resolve the conflict today. The goal today is for you both to share your expectations around money so you can start working towards resolution.

Overcoming conflicts around money is an important step to growing your relationship into the healthy marriage you desire but you also want to learn how to avoid conflicts around money. If there isn't a specific conflict you need to resolve, take some time to discuss your expectations around money. Take some time together to identify all your needs and goals that require money to meet. When you find places where your expectations are not the same, take the time to discuss those un-expectations and figure out how you will adjust expectations together so that you can avoid future conflicts around money.

CHAPTER 17

WHERE DO THE PUZZLE PIECES FIT?: GENDER ROLES OR JUST YOUR ROLES?

Another place where un-expectations can create significant conflict is in the arena of roles. By roles, we mean both how gender roles affect your view of marriage and how responsibilities are distributed in the household. These of course are both related. How you define masculinity and femininity affects how you define which roles are the responsibility of a husband or a wife.

Jen met with a woman in her early twenties who recently became engaged. She and her fiance are wonderful people and they are very sweet with each other. When the woman told Jen that she wanted "a biblical marriage," Jen held in a chuckle. She took a sip of coffee, and smiled. "Which kind? Abraham and Sarah, where he pretends to be her brother and almost marries her off to other men? Jacob and Leah and Rachel - jealous polygamy at its finest with sisters? How about the ideal woman of Proverbs 31 - but then again, she works outside the home." So what about your marriage? You can have a thriving marriage that incorporates the good advice and principles of the Bible as well as heeding its cautionary tales of those who don't have thriving marriages. But how is this achieved? What does it really look like?

We have found this particular topic of gender roles or who does what very difficult in premarital counseling. Not because it is uncomfortable to talk about, but rather because most engaged couples have an unrealistically romantic view. When we ask an engaged couple who will be responsible for household chores, the answer is universally, "We will both do everything."

"We both will do everything," sounds nice, but is romantic and unrealistic. You both can't do everything. While it looks great in commercials trying to sell cleaning products, you both can't do the dishes, do the laundry, mop the floor, or the hundreds of other household chores that must be done together every time all the time. First, you'd be constantly bumping into each other and getting in each other's way. Second, it's horribly inefficient and would prevent you from doing things that you really want to do together because your time would be filled doing chores.

Presuming you could or did do "everything together" happily when you first got married, adding children to your family creates a whole other dynamic that throws the idea into turmoil. When the first baby enters the picture, there are new tasks that need to be considered. Your energy and focus change dramatically. If you already have children, you know that roles and responsibilities necessarily change when a baby enters the equation.

As you continue in marriage, things will constantly change. As things change, roles change as well. Some changes are very definitive and have long lasting effects on your marriage. When we first got married, Bryon was a part-time youth pastor in a church about 45 minutes from our condo and Jen was working full-time in a law firm a few minutes down the road. The chores were divided pretty evenly at that time. About the time our daughter was born, Bryon took a full-time job at a church right down the street from where we lived while Jen started her own law practice. Jen was working from home limited hours as she built her firm. At that time, she bore more of the burden of household chores because she was home more and working fewer hours. Over time Jen's practice grew. As her practice grew and Bryon changed jobs and pursued different goals the balance shifted. As we write this book, Jen's practice has grown to the point that it requires more of her attention. Together, we decided that Bryon would focus more on writing, building a new ministry, and his military career. Bryon is no longer working full-time outside the home and now he is much more involved in the children's schools and taking care of things at home. Jen still does many household tasks but the balance has shifted and Bryon takes care of a lot more of the domestic responsibilities than he ever has before.

Your Mission Should You Choose to Accept It

The issue regarding roles is not really who does what. The issue is not how roles are assigned. It's not about who does what work. It's about how you decide it. You walked into marriage with expectations regarding who would do what in the marriage. Like all expectations in marriage, they come from a myriad of sources. While the sources of the expectations are the same, the impact in this arena is often greater. While money may be the most common source of marital conflict, defining roles may be a close second.

When you got married, you had expectations of what husbands', wives', mothers', and fathers' roles are in the marriage. Unless you had a very forceful counselor or mentor, you didn't talk much about that in premarital counseling. How well has that worked out for you? Have the two of you naturally fallen into the roles as you expected? We're guessing probably not. That doesn't necessarily mean that you've had major conflicts with each other, but we're guessing that reality and expectations have not always matched up.

Roles in the Bible

The first thing that is important to note is that the Bible never assigns specific roles to husbands and wives. Now some of you might be disputing that statement right now. What about Ephesians 5:22-33? Some churches use that passage to assign marital roles based on gender. Let's look at that passage and see what roles are assigned.

To fully understand the passage, we need to start earlier. A lot earlier. Ephesians 5:22-33 actually provides an application on how we should live based on the earlier argument in the letter. The argument actually starts all the way back in chapter 1. The foundation of everything Paul writes is the fact that we are saved by the grace of God and now have a new status before God and in the world as the community of the redeemed.

> In him we have redemption through his blood, the forgiveness of our trespasses, according to the riches of his grace that he lavished on us in all wisdom and insight. Ephesians 1:7-8

> In Christ we too have been claimed as God's own possession, since we were predestined according to the one purpose of him who accomplishes all things according to the counsel of his will so that we, who were the first to set our hope on Christ, would be to the praise of his glory. Ephesians 1:11-12

He goes on to describe the new life that we have in Christ through faith in him.

> And although you were dead in your transgressions and sins, in which you formerly lived according to this world's present path, according to the ruler of the kingdom of the air, the ruler of the spirit that is now energizing the sons of disobedience, among whom all of us also formerly lived out our lives in the cravings of our flesh, indulging the desires of the flesh and the mind, and were by nature children of wrath even as the rest …

> But God, being rich in mercy, because of his great love with which he loved us, even though we were dead in transgressions, made us alive together with Christ—by grace you are saved! (Ephesians 2:1-4)

The focus in the first part of Ephesians 2 is how we individually have new lives in Christ. Jesus didn't, however, leave individual Christians on earth when he ascended. He left a church; a community, "And I tell you that you are Peter, and on this rock I will build my *church*, and the gates of Hades will not overpower it" (Matthew 16:18 emphasis added). Paul describes this new corporate life as gentiles joining the people of Israel and receiving a new corporate identity.

> So then you are no longer foreigners and noncitizens, but you are fellow citizens with the saints and members of God's household, because you have been built on the foundation of the apostles and prophets, with Christ Jesus himself as the cornerstone. In him the whole building, being joined together, grows into a holy temple in the Lord, in whom you also are being built together into a dwelling place of God in the Spirit. Ephesians 2:19-22

The first two chapters of Ephesians is all about Christian identity in Christ. There is a transition in chapter three where Paul describes his role in the spreading of the gospel.

Starting in Ephesians 3, Paul describes how he is called by God to share the gospel with gentiles so that they have the ability to have this new identity in Christ. That the gentiles may be saved. As the Apostle to the Gentiles (Romans 11:13), Paul has a special concern for and feels a special obligation to the gentile Christians. This obligation leads him to pray that:

- Gentile Christians will be strengthened by the Holy Spirit (Ephesians 3:16).
- Christ will be in their hearts (Ephesians 3:17).
- They will comprehend the magnitude of Christ's love for them (Ephesians 3:18-19).

Stick with us here! Starting in Ephesians 4, Paul gets very practical. For the rest of the letter he describes how Christians ought to live in light of their status as the redeemed, their new life individually and corporately, and the hopes that Paul has for them as they grow in their faith.

Paul starts with a laundry list of interpersonal character traits that are required to live "worthy of [our] calling" in Christ: "I, therefore, the prisoner for the Lord, urge you to live worthily of the calling with which you have been called, with all humility and gentleness, with patience, bearing with one another in love, making every effort to keep the unity of the Spirit in the bond of peace (Ephesians 4:1-2). He goes on to describe how God has given the church the gift of certain individuals who will help us grow in our faith and become the community that God intends:

> It was he that gave some as apostles, some as prophets, some as evangelists, and some as pastors and teachers, to equip the saints for the work of the ministry that is to build up the body of Christ, until we attain the unity of the faith and the knowledge of the Son of God - a mature person, attaining to the measure of Christ's full stature. Ephesians 4:11-15

God has given the church the resources it needs to live in unity and accomplish his will on earth.

Because God has given us all the resources we need to live the lives to which he has called us, we must change our way of living. We must live godly, holy lives distinct from the culture around us. "So I say this, and insist in the Lord, that you no longer live as the Gentiles do, in the futility of their thinking" (Ephesians 4:17). Paul offers another list. This list is a list of expectations on how we should live:

- Be honest. (Ephesians 4:25)
- In our anger do not sin. (Ephesians 4:26)
- Work for our needs and share what we have. (Ephesians 4:27)
- Use our words to build up those around us. (Ephesians 4:29)
- Be kind, compassionate, and forgiving (Ephesians 4:32)

In chapter five, Paul continues this theme of how we should now live in light of who we are in Christ. We should be loving which is displayed by our purity, sexual and otherwise (Ephesians 5:1), and by our language which should reflect Christ in everything we say (Ephesians 5:2). "For you can be confident of this one thing: that no person who is immoral, impure, or greedy (such a person is an idolater) has any inheritance in the kingdom of Christ and God" (Ephesians 5:5).

Now we *finally* get to the place in Ephesians particularly relevant to the topic of marital roles. Notice that up to this point the only roles listed were those who were given to the church as resources to help the church become what God intends: the apostles, prophets, evangelists, pastors, and teachers (Ephesians 4:11). The entire exhortation discusses character traits that everyone should have as Christians, *not roles* Christians should practice. The final exhortation is for all Christians to submit "to one another out of reverence for Christ" (Ephesians 5:21). This is part of how Christians are to live as wise rather than unwise people (Ephesians 5:15).

The relevant passage is worth reading completely here so that we have the appropriate context:

> Wives, submit to your husbands as to the Lord, because the husband is the head of the wife as also Christ is the head of the church—he himself being the savior of the body. But as the church submits to Christ, so also wives should submit to their husbands in everything. Husbands, love your wives just as Christ loved the church and gave himself for her to sanctify her by cleansing her with the washing of the water by the word, so that he may present the church to himself as glorious—not having a stain or wrinkle, or any such blemish, but holy and blameless. In the same way husbands ought to love their wives as their own bodies. He who loves his wife loves himself. For no one has ever hated his own body but he feeds it and takes care of it, just as Christ also does the church, for we are members of his body. ***For this reason a man will leave his father and mother and will be joined to his wife, and the two will become one flesh.*** Ephesians 5:22-31, *emphasis original to translation indicating the quote from Genesis 2:24*

There are no roles anywhere in that passage. Nowhere does it define housekeeping as women's work or mowing the lawn as men's work. The purpose of this passage is to exhort husbands and wives to *live in unity* in the same way that Paul exhorts all Christians to live in unity.

What about that word "submit" in verse 22? "Wives, submit to your husbands as to the Lord." Well in some of the earliest texts, that word isn't even there. Many of the earliest manuscripts don't have a verb there at all.

The lack of a verb in that clause is not strange when you consider how Paul writes and how Greek was written at the time. The verb was implied. The whole sentence points back to verse 21 where Paul says that all Christians should submit to each other "out of reverence for Christ". The whole point is that Christians should live in unity. Christian unity should impact every aspect or Christian life, so in verse 22 Paul instructs husbands and wives that they should live in unity in their homes. The rest of chapter 5 and the beginning of chapter 6 go on to exhort households to live in unity.

Paul also wrote in Galatians 3:28 that "there is no longer Jew or Gentile, slave or free, male and female. For you are all one in Christ Jesus." We all stand shoulder to shoulder at the foot of the cross. Paul instructs us in Ephesians how to live as Christians but not as men and women or husband and wife.

As you can now see, the Bible does not define roles in marriage. The Bible is silent about who should do what around the house. The Bible doesn't even say whose responsibility it is to work outside the home. The Bible does not define roles. Rather, it defines how you should live fulfilling whatever role you are in. The priority is that you love each other and live in unity. Whether you have structured your family like the TV shows from the 1950s with dad working outside the home and mom keeping house; whether you are a dual income family; whether mom works outside the home while dad cares for the children; or any other structure you can imagine, all are biblical if you love each other and strive for unity in your home.

Deciding Roles

If the Bible does not define roles in marriage, how should roles be defined?

However you want, there is no rule.

There are no roles that are specifically defined as husbands' roles. There are no roles specifically defined as wives' roles. That being said, it does matter how roles are defined. As you decide who will fulfill what roles you must define it in a way that is loving and draws you closer together. According to Ephesians, your goal is mutual love and unity as you determine the roles that you will each fulfill in your marriage.

With that in mind, here are some ideas that may help you define the roles for your family. First let's talk about gender differentiation. While it is clear that there are very obvious biological differences between men and women that should be acknowledged and respected, our biological differences do not necessarily require different roles. Gender roles are defined more culturally than biologically. The culture in which you grew up taught you what is masculine and what is feminine. In most cases, those roles are morally neutral. While we acknowledge that there are cultures in which gender roles are defined in a way that is abusive, that is not the common experience for most people in the United States. In the United States, affluent families are more likely to have mom stay at home while dad works. Lower income families are more likely to be dual income. Rural families are more likely to follow "traditional" 1950s-ish gender roles than urban families. These are all biblically acceptable and morally neutral.

The important point here is that your culture has defined gender roles for you. As a couple, you may be comfortable with this and will follow the general roles you were assigned by culture. If you are both comfortable with this, then you should happily live out those roles without any concern about what you see on television or what others think about your household.

One or both of you, however, may not be comfortable with the gender roles assigned by your culture. If that is the case, discuss your concerns together and determine what works best for your family. You should be aware that if the roles you define in your household differ substantially from how your culture defines gender roles it will be noticed. You should be aware that people will think your family odd because you are different from what they expect. It would be wise to be prepared for how you will respond in those situations. *But, that is ok!* There is no right and wrong when defining gender roles as long as it is done in love and to bring unity in your family.

As we discussed earlier in this chapter, we have changed how we define the roles in our marriage based on the context. When our daughter was born, our family followed more traditional gender roles. Jen was the primary caregiver for our daughter and the primary one maintaining the home while Bryon primarily worked outside the home, even while Jen was building her law practice. Years later as Jen's law practice grew the roles slowly shifted. Today, Bryon is far more involved in maintaining the home, volunteering at the children's schools, and caring for the children while Jen is working more. It was not a complete 180 degree shift. Jen is still very involved in maintaining the home, the children's school, and caring for the children. Bryon, however, handles a lot more so that Jen is more free to focus on her law practice. Yet, Jen must manage everything when Bryon is out of town for military duty or ministry conferences. Then, her time devoted to the household and kids increases.

In reality, the core issue regarding defining roles has very little to do with gender and has a lot to do with fairness. In marriage, conflicts occur in the area of roles not because of the roles themselves but the perceived fairness regarding how roles are assigned. "Researchers have found that in dual-earner couples, both husbands and wives who feel they're doing more than their fair share of the housework are less happily married and more likely to divorce. ... Spouses who believe they're getting the short end of the deal may experience depression, distress, anger, or rage."[55] On the other hand, couples where each feels like they got the better end of the deal - as expressed to Jen by one of her mentors in law and life - are grateful to the other and happy in their roles.

Here we get to the crux of the issue. Ultimately the health of your marriage is not determined by who fulfills which roles. The health of your marriage will be determined by how fairly you feel the roles are assigned. There are two actions you can take to help ensure your marriage is healthy in this area. First, talk together about the roles you fill. Discuss honestly about your feelings regarding the division of labor for housekeeping, meals, childcare, and all the other roles that make your household run. Second, focus on how you can serve your spouse. Think back to chapter 13 of this book (Serving Each Other). The roles you fulfill in your marriage should be fulfilled with an attitude of service towards your spouse and move towards unity. When both of you focus on serving each other, the issue of fairness becomes moot.

Jen often describes true friendship as mutual favors where no one is

---

[55] *Preparing Couples for Love and Marriage*

keeping track. That is even more relevant in marriage. Marriage is mutual service where no one is keeping track of who is serving whom because the goal is to grow closer together.

Conclusion

Conflicts often arise in marriage over the area of roles. Specifically, conflict arises around who will be responsible for what to make the household function. While it has been argued in many Christian circles that the Bible defines marital roles, that is not true. The Bible does not define marital roles but rather defines how we should behave while we fulfill the roles we play in marriage. We must submit to each other in love. The goal is for us to live in unity in our marriages. After all, in marriage we have become one.

Action step:

To overcome and avoid conflict over roles in your marriage, first discuss how you feel about how the roles have been defined in your marriage. If you are unhappy about how the roles are defined, discuss it together. Remember, rarely is the issue which roles a person fulfills but rather the perceived inequity in how the roles are distributed. Second, remember the goal is oneness. The goal is unity. Rather than focusing on who should do what, focus instead on serving one another in love.

This week:

- Make a list of the roles you each play in your marriage.
- Discuss how you feel about the roles you play.
- Considering the roles you each play in your marriage, come up with a way to serve your spouse this week. Focus totally on serving, not on who ought to do things or what is fair based on your present circumstances.

CHAPTER 18

CONFLICT GETS PHYSICAL: MANAGING YOUR ANGER

All conflicts get physical. No, we don't mean violent. We're not saying that all conflicts result in physical rage, and in marriage, physical violence should never happen. All conflict does, however, cause a physiological response. The human body responds physically and predictably to conflict. Any sort of conflict you face triggers a hormonal and physical response in your body. It doesn't matter if it's a conflict at work, with friends, or your spouse; your body is going to respond physically to the conflict.

The fact that everyone responds physically to conflict is unavoidable. There is no way to prevent normal physical responses to conflict. In fact, you don't want to prevent those physical responses because they are an important part of how your body gives you information about your environment. The physical response to conflict, when given the appropriate attention, will help you to healthily manage the conflicts you face.

Managing conflict is the goal. We've spent several chapters talking about potential causes of conflict and how to mitigate those factors. Here's a little secret: you *will* have conflict. Conflict is unavoidable. Conflict is even an important part of you becoming one. Conflict is healthy in marriage when managed in a healthy manner. Understanding the physical aspect of conflict will help you to manage conflict in a healthy manner.

The Physiology of Conflict

In chapter eight, we talked about the limbic system and how the part of our mind that controls emotion responds to stimulus before our conscious mind is able to respond. It also informs our conscious mind on how we should respond. Have you ever lost your temper? If you answered no you are either lying or you need to check your pulse. We all have lost our tempers at some point.

Losing your temper is actually a normal human response to certain stimuli. We're not saying it is the healthiest or best response, but it is normal. Losing your temper is often an immediate response to the limbic system flooding your body with specific hormones intended to prepare you to defend yourself. The hormones released when we are angry are the same ones released when we feel we are in danger. When our bodies are flooded with these hormones, we sometimes lash out without thinking. We say or do things without thinking in response to the reaction our limbic system made to a given stimulus. No one has broken a hand against a wall because it was a well-reasoned thought out response to a situation. No one has thrown a book, or shoe, or other item close at hand because it made logical sense to do so. No one has directed profanity or other hurtful language at their spouse because wisdom dictated that was the best response. None of these responses are controlled by our conscious brains. They are responses to the hormones released by our limbic system.

People will often say in response to such actions, "I wasn't thinking." Though that response should not be used to excuse bad behavior, it is still literally true. The actor wasn't thinking. Instead, it was an immediate response to stimulus. "Our brains are wired in such a way as to influence us to act before we can properly consider the consequences of our actions."[56]

Anger is unavoidable. It is a natural part of the human condition. One of the triggers to anger is interpersonal conflict. What happens to us physically when we get angry? Anger is triggered in the area of the limbic system called the amygdala. We experience some stimulus and that stimulus triggers an anger response. In marriage, it is usually a response to one of our un-expectations. The immediate response is for the amygdala

---

[56] "Physiology of Anger", MentalHelp.net, https://www.mentalhelp.net/anger/physiology, accessed Dec 26, 2019

to tell your adrenal glands to release specific neurotransmitters. These are the same neurotransmitters that trigger the fight or flight instinct.[57] These neurotransmitters increase our awareness and responsiveness: they put us "on edge." As a result, our bodies are flooded with glucose. Our bodies are now ready to respond. Our muscles are prepared for action. Our attention narrows focusing on that which is causing our anger.[58]

You will notice this happening as the rest of your body responds to the situation or other person's actions triggering your anger. The first thing you might notice is your muscles tense as you get ready for action. Many people will feel their fists and jaw clench. Some may notice a tightening in their shoulders or their gut. All of this is your muscles preparing for action. You may also notice that you're breathing heavier as your body works to get more oxygen in your system. Your heart rate will also increase. You may feel your heart pounding in your chest or your pulse racing. You may also feel your face get flushed as your blood races through your body. At this point, your body is ready for action. The adrenaline coursing through your veins is there to keep you at this heightened state of readiness so that you have the endurance necessary to deal with the situation. This makes it harder to calm down and compose yourself because your body is ready to fight.

Conflict comes with emotion and sometimes that emotion is anger. It is unavoidable. When we get angry, our bodies respond before we can even think through exactly what we're angry about or why we're angry. Knowing that our bodies respond to the emotions related to conflict in a specific and predictable way will help us to manage those physiological reactions and successfully navigate the conflict we are facing.

We've noticed that in recent years, the American church has taken the position that anger is somehow wrong, or if taken to an extreme, teaches that anger is sin. We disagree with the church teaching that anger, in and of itself, is sin. Scripture specifically teaches that anger is not sin. What

---

[57] ibid.

[58] La Velle Hendricks, et. al., "The Effects of Anger on the Brain and Body", *National Forum Journal of Counseling and Addiction*, Vol. 2, Num. 1, (2013) http://www.nationalforum.com/Electronic%20Journal%20Volumes/Hendricks,%20 LaVelle%20The%20Effects%20of%20Anger%20on%20the%20Brain%20and%20 Body%20NFJCA%20V2%20N1%202013.pdf, accessed Jul 15, 2020.

you choose to do with the emotion of anger determines whether you sin or don't sin.

Paul writes, "Be angry and do not sin; do not let the sun go down on the cause of your anger" (Ephesians 4:26). We deal with the first part of this verse here and the second part later in this chapter. Paul notes that you are able to be angry, but directs us to not sin. The New Living Translation puts it this way, "don't sin by letting anger control you." Again, don't let your emotions control you.

Is your life characterized by your anger? Are you an angry person or do you merely experience anger sometimes? Paul notes in Galatians 5 the fruit of the Spirit is "love, joy, peace, patience, kindness, goodness, faithfulness, gentleness, and self-control. Against such things there is no law" (Galatians 5:22-23). Anger is not present here. You should not be known by your anger (i.e. as a perpetually angry person) but you can and will experience anger. Keep it under control.

As we finish editing this book, we have been saddened and angered by systemic racism and the death of George Floyd caused by a former Minneapolis police officer acting in the line of duty. We are also saddened and angry about both police and protestors killed in recent protests across the country. Sometimes, anger can be a godly call to action. Nehemiah used his anger to respond to the people of Israel being charged interest on loans, which was contrary to Jewish law (Nehemiah 5:6-7). Nehemiah in his anger did not sin. Instead, He stopped this practice. We also recall Jesus in the temple, braiding cords into a whip, turning over tables, yelling, and driving money changers of the Temple (John 2:13-18). Jesus was angry but he certainly did not sin. His zeal for his Father's house caused his anger and he used his anger to see to it that his Father's house was treated as a place of worship rather than a marketplace.

James instructs us to "Let every person be quick to listen, slow to speak, slow to anger. For human anger does not accomplish God's righteousness" (James 1:21-22). In conflicts with your spouse, your anger is more likely than not to be "human anger" rather than a holy anger. We believe that God understands your anger and directs you to rely on him to respond to that anger in holy ways rather than sinful ways. Manage this human anger well and by doing so, do not sin. But how do you manage anger, especially when it causes a physical response?

Managing Reactions to Conflict

When you notice that your body is responding in anger to the conflict your first step is to deescalate. At this point, we're not talking about deescalating the conflict or disagreement itself. At this point, you need to deescalate *your reaction* to the situation. You need to take steps to slow your body's reaction so that your frontal cortex can regain control over your decision making. The way we describe this to our children is that you need to control your emotions and not let your emotions control you. You can't stop feeling emotions. In fact, you don't want to stop feeling emotions; it's part of what makes us human. You do, however, want to control how you react to your emotions. Jen often says that it's important to respond rather than react; in this sense, a response is thought out, decisive and wise while a reaction is quick, rash, and unbridled.

The first step is to be aware of the warning signs that happen when you begin to get angry. While the physiological reaction to anger is generally the same for everyone, the specific response is unique to the individual. Your specific responses to those general reactions were conditioned by the culture around you. For example, in America, it is more culturally acceptable for men to lash out in anger than for women to lash out in anger. Your responses were also conditioned by your family. How was anger displayed in your home? Did people yell? Did your dad grit his teeth? Did your mom get physically agitated and start moving around the house?

One of the things that happens to Bryon is he gets physically agitated. One time, not long after we moved to Ann Arbor, we got into an argument about something. Honestly, we can't remember what the argument was about, but it was intense and took a while for us to resolve the issue. At some point we came to an impasse and decided that we needed to take a break from the conversation because we weren't getting anywhere. Jen went downstairs to the family room and turned on the TV. Bryon stayed on the main floor of the house. Since he was still angry and agitated, he needed to do something to work out the extra energy. He, therefore, spent the next couple of hours cleaning. He loaded the dishwasher, cleaned the kitchen counters, took out the trash, cleaned both bathrooms, and mopped the floors. The main floor of the house was beautiful, and Bryon had worked out the anger to the point where he could discuss the issue rationally. During that same time, Jen was able to unwind and we were able to resolve whatever the conflict was we were facing. Don't worry, Jen does not intentionally provoke Bryon to anger to utilize his mad house cleaning skills.

Whatever it is, you have to figure out what works for you to manage your physiological reactions to anger. The first thing that we recommend you do is go to the gym. We don't mean go to the gym when you're in the middle of a conflict (Although that would help, too. It's something Jen does to blow off steam, usually having to do with a difficult litigation case). Instead, go to the gym before you get into the conflict. Good physical health, particularly cardiovascular health, will help you manage your anger. Good cardiovascular health helps your body recover from stressful situations. A healthy heart slows down faster and someone with good cardiovascular health will experience their blood pressure recover faster. These things will allow your body to recover more quickly from anger and conflict.

This is one of the primary reasons the Air Force has a physical fitness test. As a member of the Michigan Air National Guard, Bryon has to take and pass a physical fitness test annually. The current Air Force Physical Fitness Test (AFPFT) consists of a waist measurement, push-ups, sit-ups, and a 1½ mile run. The Air Force has a very different primary mission from the other branches of the US military, especially the Army and Marine Corps. Most airmen will never be in a firefight with the enemy. Most will not have to do a forced march carrying gear through harsh terrain. Our primary mission is tied to an airbase. Our jobs are generally confined to this very specific location. The farthest we might have to run is about 100 yards if the base is under attack from some sort of indirect fire. There are certain career fields, such as security forces, that directly engage the enemy, but most do not.

Since the main wartime job for most airmen is on base sitting behind a computer or repairing aircraft within the relative safety of the base, many airmen have argued to Bryon that the AFPFT is irrelevant to what they do. While it is true that during combat operations no airmen will need to do push-ups or sit-ups, and few will have to run 1½ miles, the physical conditioning is vital to their successful execution of the mission. Simply being deployed, away from family and living in conditions harsher than home, raises airmen's stress level. Add to that the additional stress of launching aircraft at a very high rate, or performing all the other tasks necessary to keep an airbase running at a very high level. Their bodies are responding very differently than they do at home. Now imagine that they are receiving indirect fire, or a suicide bomber just attacked the base gate, the stress level of these airmen has spiked. In the midst of all of this, they have to accomplish their tasks at a high level to accomplish the mission. No one on base gets to slack off. Everyone is needed to make the mission happen. Those who are physically fit will be able to respond to the stress in a positive way and press through to make things happen. Bryon tells his airmen that is the reason they need to pass the AFPFT. The need to be physically fit is not so they can do their job under normal conditions. They need to be physically fit so they can do their absolute best job on their absolute worst day.

Now if you're following the other advice we've given in this book, marital conflict will not feel like you're in a warzone. No, Pat Benatar's song "Love is a Battlefield" should never apply to your marriage. We all, however, need to be able to do our best thinking on the worst day of our marriage. We need to be able to handle conflict in the best possible way in the worst marital conflict. Being physically fit will be helpful in managing your physiological reactions to conflict.

Ok, being physically fit will prepare you for managing your physical reactions to marital conflict, but what about in the midst of the conflict? What do you do to manage your emotional reactions when the conflict is happening? When you start feeling the reactions that we discussed above respond to those reactions. When you notice yourself physically responding in anger do something about it. The first thing we recommend is trying some simple relaxation techniques. The best way to relax is to take a deep breath. Try it now. Inhale deeply. Exhale slowly. Did you notice the stress release? The very act of taking a deep breath forces your muscles to respond in a more relaxed manner. Think about it. What happens when someone startles you? All your muscles get tight. Your whole body stiffens up. Your heart starts beating a little faster. Ok, now what do you do when you realize you're safe? You take a deep breath right? It's relaxing. It's a natural way to release the stress that has built up. When you're running for your life or fighting to defend yourself, you don't take deep breaths. You breathe heavy and fast to get as much oxygen into your blood as possible. Taking a deep breath will begin to help you relax.

Another thing a deep breath will do is slow you down. That second or two you just took to breathe deeply has given your frontal cortex time to be more aware of the situation. In that brief moment, your brain may come up with a better way to respond to the situation than that immediate emotional response.

Once you take a deep breath, the next thing is to consciously relax your muscles. People notice their muscles tightening in different ways. Some notice their jaws clenching. Others ball up their hands into fists. Whatever it is for you when you're in an argument with your spouse and notice your muscles tightening after you take that deep breath, relax your muscles. Unclench your jaw. Open up your hands. Consciously relax your muscles. Like taking a deep breath, relaxing your muscles will help your body calm down and allow your conscious mind better control over your body. Your limbic system will respond to what you are doing physically.

There will be times when one or both of you are too fired up to resolve the conflict you are facing in the moment. No matter how many deep breaths, or how hard you try to relax your muscles, you still won't be able to calm your body down. In those instances, trying to resolve the conflict in the moment will probably do more harm than good. Your reactions will be emotional and more likely hurtful. At times like that it's hard to remember that the goal is to strengthen your relationship. The emotional goal becomes to win the fight. The best thing to do when things are that heated is to take a break and walk away from the conflict.

It's ok to walk away from a fight and come back to address the conflict later. Remember, in situations like this, you are not walking away from each other. You are walking away from a fight so that you can come back together later and healthily resolve the conflict. When you take time away from each other, we intend this to be hours, not a day or days. It is also important how you use this time to relax and gain perspective to come back together and resolve the conflict together. This time apart is not time to feed addictions or bad mouth your spouse to others.

It is also important that you learn more about how you and your spouse react to conflict. You can then honor how you both react. If needed, ask to take time to step away. You may need to ask your spouse if they need to take some time. If your spouse needs to breathe, allow the space to let them do so. If you need to adjust your body, such as unclenching your jaw, ask your spouse for the space to do so.

When your spouse asks for space to work out their emotions, give it to them. They are not asking for space from you. They are asking for space from the argument. If you want a thriving marriage, you need to allow each other the opportunity to work through things together.

When taking a break from a conflict, it's ok to take the time you need to get the composure you need to resolve the conflict. In the example above of Bryon cleaning the house while he was angry, Bryon took several hours cleaning the house and processing his emotions to the point where he could calmly address this issue at hand. The important thing to remember is that the goal is to relieve the stress your body is experiencing and bring your adrenaline back down. Rehearsing the fight over and over again in your mind will only spin you up more. Your adrenaline will keep pumping and you will stay in fight or flight mode. Your body is designed to keep you functioning at maximum physical capacity until the perceived threat is gone or you are completely exhausted. Your goal here is to hack the system. Your body is responding to the conflict as a threat and you need to convince your limbic system that you are safe. Once that happens you will be able to resolve the conflict you are facing.

Another thing to ask yourself and your spouse is whether your marriage is safe. Your marriage should be a safe relationship where you grow holy and healthy together. It should provide the safety to fail and the safety to inspire curiosity to try new ways to grow in holiness. If your marriage can grow in safety to each other, focus on growing that kind of marriage.

Letting the Sun Go Down

Some have argued that the Bible says we must resolve conflict before we go to sleep. The argument comes from Ephesians. Ephesians 4:26 says, "Be angry and do not sin; do not let the sun go down on the cause of your anger." The NIV translates the second half of that verse as, "Do not let the sun go down while you are still angry." First, that is really good advice. The longer you are angry, the harder it is to resolve a conflict. It is a good practice to resolve conflicts as quickly as possible. Your relationship is stronger by resolving conflict not by being in conflict.

The passage should not, however, be interpreted as a command. "Be angry and do not sin" is a direct quote from the Greek translation of Psalm 4:4. It seems that this phrase, in the time of Paul, may have become proverbial, meaning be angry but do not act sinfully while angry.[59] "Do not let the sun go down on the cause of your anger," appears to be a proverbial statement as well.[60] Paul's point is that the longer you sit in your anger, the more likely you are to act out in sin. We should not marinate in anger or other negative emotions. We should not soak up the negative emotions allowing ourselves to be forever changed by them in bitterness. It is, therefore, a good practice to resolve conflict before you go to bed so that the relationship can be stronger.

It, however, is not sin to go to sleep before resolving conflict. In this case, Paul is speaking proverbially providing good advice on how to live the Christian life, not communicating a command from God. It may, sometimes, be better to sleep on an issue overnight to gain perspective so that the conflict can be resolved. Even so, the best practice is to resolve conflicts quickly and restore the relationship, which is what Jesus said in Matthew 5:25. So the sun may go down on your conflict so that you both can gain perspective but the sun should not go down on your commitment to each other and to resolve the conflict. At your best, you should be able to still enjoy each other's company and table the conflict to be discussed the next day. Make sure to promptly then address the conflict; it is healthy to address the conflict but not healthy to avoid it.

Conclusion

Conflict always affects us physiologically. Our bodies respond in predictable ways when we have conflicts in our marriage. Unfortunately, our physical responses to conflict can make it more difficult for us to resolve conflict in a healthy way. Developing our ability to predict our

---

[59] Harold W. Hoehner, *Ephesians*, (Grand Rapids, MI: Baker Publishing Group, 2002), Kindle Locations 12585-12587
[60] ibid.

physical responses to conflict can help us mitigate that response and resolve conflict in a healthy manner.

The first way to mitigate our physical responses to conflict is to maintain a healthy lifestyle. Being physically fit helps our body adapt to and recover from the physical effects of conflict more quickly. This can help us better manage the conflict as our body is better equipped to handle it.

While in conflict, simple relaxation techniques can help us mitigate our physical response so that we can resolve the conflict in a healthy manner. The most effective technique is to simply take a deep breath. A deep breath will help us relax and give our conscious mind time to catch up with our limbic system. We will, then, have better control of how we interact during the conflict. Consciously relaxing our tense muscles will also help us overcome our limbic response to conflict.

Finally, some conflicts cannot be resolved immediately because one or both of us are unable to overcome the emotional response to the conflict. In these situations, it is best to take a break from the argument and come back later to resolve the conflict together. Taking a break helps us to work through our emotional response giving us better perspectives.

Action steps:

- If you don't already have one, develop a fitness plan that will help you build and maintain your physical fitness. A good way to start is going for a family walk after dinner. That little step will give you all time to connect and go a long way to building a healthy lifestyle. Don't forget that diet and sleep are important to a healthy lifestyle.
- Reflect on and discuss how each of you respond to conflict physically? How can you and your spouse best support each other in mitigating your physical responses to anger?
- Take some time to discuss how you can communicate that you need to take a break during an argument.

CHAPTER 19

STRATEGIC INITIATIVE: TOOLS TO RESOLVE CONFLICT WELL

So far we've discussed the major causes of conflict, how to mitigate those factors to avoid unnecessary conflict, and the physiology of how our bodies respond to conflict when it happens. As we get close to the end of this book, it's time to look at strategies for resolving conflict. Conflict is inevitable. As we discussed earlier in this section, you are going to face un-met, un-shared, and un-voiced expectations. This is unavoidable. Since conflict is unavoidable, how do you resolve conflict in a way that is going to help you have a thriving marriage that lasts a lifetime? Before we get into some strategies to resolve conflict, let's talk about the purpose of conflict.

Conflict Isn't All Bad

Conflict is not all bad. Conflict does not cause divorce or unhappy marriages. Conflict is not a problem in marriage. Mishandled and unresolved conflict is the problem. Mishandled and unresolved conflict causes unhappy marriages that can lead to divorce. Preventing mishandled and unresolved conflict is easier when you understand the purpose behind conflict in marriage.

Conflict is actually an important part of a thriving marriage. To explain why, let's review what we've discussed in earlier chapters about the purpose of marriage. In chapter one we listed three purposes for marriage:

1. To experience the mature fulfilling love that God intends for you
2. To grow to be more like Jesus
3. To represent God to the people around you.

In chapters two and three we discussed that this happens in marriage more than in any other relationship because marriage is fundamentally different from any other relationship you experience. Through marriage, two people become one couple fundamentally changing their identity while also retaining their separate uniqueness. In chapter four we talked about how the real goal of marriage is to become more holy. Chapter five and the following chapters described how this goal is accomplished by the process of becoming one.

Conflict, when neither mishandled nor neglected, actually helps in the process of becoming one. Conflict in marriage highlights important things to becoming one and becoming more holy. Some conflicts highlight ways in which the two of you still have not become one. These conflicts involve differences in how you live as a couple. The core issues in these conflicts are how you make decisions together, goals for the family, and the like. Other conflicts revolve around issues of personal holiness. This conflict reveals flaws in your character that God is working out. They often address how you're treating your spouse or children, how you're handling money, or other areas of pride, selfishness, and insecurity.

The purpose of conflict in marriage is to resolve the core issues that cause the conflict. In other words, resolving conflict helps to resolve the issues that caused the conflict in the first place. Resolving these issues will build oneness in your marriage or help you develop your character. Often, they do both. In other words, conflict is an essential part of marriage that helps to fulfill the purpose of marriage.

When Conflict Goes Bad

Conflict goes bad when it is mishandled or unresolved. Conflict is mishandled or unresolved when the purpose and value of conflict is misunderstood. There are two common ways when this happens in a relationship. Conflict is often viewed as a competition between two opposing parties or a negative, undesirable aspect of relationships.

Conflict seen as competition leads to conflict mishandled. We've all done this before. The goal in the middle of the conflict in this situation is to win and not to resolve the conflict. In these situations there is no true communication. You're not listening to understand. You're only listening to find a point to attack and a counterargument to annihilate the other's position. The whole time you're not thinking of how to resolve the issue. You're thinking of how to prove your point. You're thinking of how to win the argument. In such arguments, one or both of you have a winner take all mentality.

A winner take all mentality will always lead to a mishandled conflict. You may win the argument. Your spouse may concede that you're right. It will not, however, bring you closer together. Ultimately, this is a selfish way to handle the conflict. You don't care about the other spouse, their feelings, or their needs. At the end of the argument, you are farther apart. The more this type of argument happens, the greater danger your marriage is in.

Jen has seen too many divorcing couples nit-pick at each other and even fight over a pot or a pan to somehow win. Their conflicts started long before anyone called a lawyer to file for divorce. They started with a pattern of a husband and a wife entering conflict with a winner take all mentality. Whether the conflicts started over which side of the family to visit for holidays, how to spend or save a work bonus, or children's activities, the breakdown of the marriage became inevitable because the conflicts were not managed properly.

Other than the winner take all mentality, avoiding conflict is another destructive way to manage conflict. When conflict is viewed as negative and undesirable, it is often avoided. The thought here is that if the conflict is avoided then there isn't a chance for it to be mishandled. Often people who avoid conflict have never or rarely seen conflict resolved. They have only seen conflict mishandled. They have only seen conflict divide people and sever relationships. Since conflict inevitably leads to an undesirable outcome, these people reason that it is better for conflict to be avoided altogether.

Conflict avoided will never be resolved. Even if the context of the conflict ends, the conflict never really resolves. The conflict festers, even if it is not longer relevant. One or both of you will have feelings left unexpressed. The un-expectations that triggered the conflict are never addressed. They remain un-expectations. Avoiding conflict communicates to each other that resolving the conflict is not valuable. It communicates the un-expectations that triggered the conflict are not relevant or important. Over time, unresolved conflicts can significantly reduce trust in your relationship. It hinders communication and drives a wedge between you.

Years ago, Jen met with a client-wife who wanted a thriving marriage but whose husband never met what she thought were reasonable standards. She was upset that he never attended church with her, yet she never invited him. She was upset when he drank heavily, but she never discussed it with him. She was upset when he stayed out late with his poker buddies, but she never told him how she felt. After this pattern had persisted over the years, the wife became fed up with her husband's behaviors. He did not and could not have known because she never told him. As far as he was concerned, his behaviors were fine and so was the marriage! So his behaviors had become the norm. Had she addressed these issues early on insteading of hiding them and letting them fester, she could have resolved these issues with her husband, or perhaps with her husband and a counselor rather than coming into Jen's office to end the marriage.

Conflict is not bad for your marriage. It goes bad when it is viewed as a competition or simply avoided. Nothing good comes from conflict that is mishandled or unresolved.

Resolving Conflict

There are almost countless books written on the subject of resolving conflict. Conflict is universal to the human condition and certainly universal in marriage. In this book, it is not our goal to exhaustively discuss conflict and how to resolve it. In the end, your marriage is unique to you and while conflict is universal, the ways that work to resolve conflict for you may not work for us. Conflict resolution is not an arithmetic problem whereby going through the precise steps correctly will always get the desired outcome. Conflict resolution is more like writing a short story. There are certain elements that are necessary but skill and practice will ultimately determine the quality and effectiveness of your conflicts. Two stories may have similar plots, settings, and characters, but no two stories are alike. We offer you three tips that will help you resolve conflict in your marriage: be kind, be clear, and be present.

Be Kind

Being kind should be an obvious point. Kindness is one of the fruits of the spirit (Galatians 5:22). As obvious as it may be, we find that couples in trouble have often stopped being kind when they are in conflict. Lack of kindness will inevitably lead to mishandled or unresolved conflict. Unkind communication or actions in conflict may lead to apparent resolution, but in reality only leads to the dominant spouse getting their own way. When there is no dominant personality or the dominant person is unable to bully their spouse into submission, the conflict ends without resolution and festers, creating a bigger problem.

As simple as be kind sounds, many people are unaware of what it means to be kind in conflict. They may never have seen an example of kindness in conflict or presume that their actions are kind. Kindness starts with presuming goodwill. We discussed this in detail in chapter 8. When you approach a conflict thinking your partner has it out for you, is trying to make things difficult for you, or doesn't care about your feelings, you will likely respond in a similar manner. But remember, you're in this together. You chose each other to be devoted to each other for the rest of your lives. You have become one flesh. Your spouse is not trying to make things difficult for you. Start by thinking the best of your spouse and you are more likely to resolve the conflict in a healthy manner. "Do not repay anyone evil for evil; consider what is good before all people" (Romans 12:17).

In chapter 10 we talked about the importance of communicating in such a way as to be heard. Kindness means speaking in a kind and gentle manner. "A gentle [kind] response turns away anger, but a harsh word stirs up wrath" (Proverbs 15:1). You need to communicate in a way that will help the other person hear the real issue. A harsh tone or harsh, demeaning language prevents your spouse from hearing the message you're sending. When your spouse is overwhelmed by the harsh emotion surrounding your words, they lose your words but remember being treated poorly. Instead of using harsh language and/or harsh tones, be kind and gentle in words and tone. Recall that a good friend of ours calls this using the "butter voice." When you want to resolve a conflict talk in the same way you would ask your mom to pass the butter at the dinner table.

Be Clear

Conflicts are almost guaranteed to be mishandled or go unresolved if there is not clarity on what the conflict is about. Specificity is valuable here. The conflict you are facing is the result of an un-expectation. Define the action and the un-expectation. Words like "always" and "never" are not helpful in resolving conflict. Say specifically what the action was that is causing the conflict and connect it to the un-expectation.

It is also important to be clear about your feelings. Recently we dealt with a conflict regarding how Jen should handle a situation with a friend who hurt her feelings. The conversation started out simply enough. Jen said that maybe she should address the issue with her friend in a certain way. She seemed to be soliciting advice on how to deal with the situation. Bryon responded, suggesting that the issue was something different from what Jen was suggesting. Bryon misread the situation. Jen was looking for support in a difficult situation, not advice on how to deal with it. In response, Jen explained to Bryon that she felt like he did not support her in dealing with this situation. Jen expected Bryon to listen and give her space to process what was going on. By trying to reframe the situation to what Bryon presumed the issue was, Bryon failed to meet Jen's expectation. That changed things immediately. Jen clearly stated how she felt at that moment. That helped Bryon understand the true issue. Jen had to leave at that point to take one of our children to school. When she returned, Bryon apologized for hurting her feelings. The conversation continued later that day. Jen continued to wrestle with how to handle the situation with her friend, but the conflict that arose from the un-expectation between us was resolved.

Be Present

There are two aspects to the principle of being present. The first is to handle conflict in the present tense. The conflict you are resolving is the conflict you are facing now. It is not helpful to rehash old conflicts. It is not useful to bring up unresolved conflicts that linger. The situation you are facing must control your attention. You can deal with other unresolved issues later. Resolve this conflict first.

Be present to your spouse. Dialogues resolve conflicts, not monologues. Be aware of your spouse. Respond to the emotions you see in their body language. Give them space to respond to what you have said. Conflict resolution done well only happens when both people are able to communicate their concerns and develop the resolution together.

Conclusion

Conflict is inevitable in marriage. While conflict is blamed for a lot of problems in marriage and the end to many marriages, conflict itself is not the problem. Mishandled and unresolved conflicts are the real problem in marriage. Conflict is actually a healthy part of marriage. It is through healthily resolved conflict that you continue to become one in marriage and become more holy. As unexpectations are addressed and handled well, you both become more united in marriage and your character flaws are addressed.

There is no simple equation to resolving conflict. Conflicts are as unique as the people in them. There are three principles, however, that help resolve conflict healthily. Be kind. Be clear. Be present.

Action step:

Discuss together:

- Before reading this chapter, what was your opinion about the purpose and value of conflict?
- What principles would you add to healthy conflict resolution for your marriage?
- Are there any mishandled or unresolved conflicts in your marriage? If so, discuss a plan to resolve them.

CHAPTER 20

THE MOST EFFECTIVE TACTIC IN THE OPERATION

This is, without a doubt, the most important chapter in this book. There is nothing more important than this in Christian marriage. As a matter of fact, there is nothing more important than this in the Christian life. The skill we are going to discuss in this chapter is, perhaps, the hardest one in life to learn. This skill, when practiced consistently, will change your marriage for the better. If you fail to practice this skill, it will be impossible for you to experience the marriage that God intends. Without this skill, you will never have a thriving marriage. It is more important than communication. It is more important than conflict resolution. It is more important than how you manage money, or in-laws, or sex.

It is forgiveness.

The health and happiness of your marriage is absolutely *limited* by your ability to forgive. It shouldn't surprise you that we place such a high value on forgiveness. Forgiveness is fundamental to Christianity. Without forgiveness, there is no Christianity. The gospel is that God loves us too much to leave us in our sin and through Christ's life, death, and resurrection, our sins are forgiven. Yet many Christians struggle with defining forgiveness and how to practice forgiveness in their own relationships.

Defining Forgiveness[61]

The word used most often for forgive in the New Testament is άφίημι (*aphiemi*). The basic idea of the word is to release, let go, or move away from. In relationships, the idea is to release someone from an obligation or debt. We use the word in the same sense with regard to finances. We say we "forgive a debt," meaning the money owed is no longer owed.

The Hebrew word from which the New Testament writers draw the idea of forgiveness is נָשָׂא (*nasa*). The basic meaning of *nasa* is to lift up or carry. It can be used in many various contexts from lifting up your hand to strike someone to lifting up your eyes in worship. Whoever came up with the name NASA (National Aeronautics and Space Administration), the name of the United States space program where astronauts are lifted up and carried into space, good on you.

When used in the context of sin, *nasa* is applied in two ways in the Old Testament. The first sense carries the idea of carrying the weight or burden of sin. It is used with the idea of the scapegoat. The scapegoat would *nasa* (carry) the sin of Israel out into the desert. The other sense in relation to sin is the idea of lifting off or removing the burden of sin. This is the sense from which we draw the concept of forgiveness. The penalty or consequence of sin is lifted off the person and carried away.[62] Clearly, the sin itself is not lifted up or carried away. The sinful act has been committed. It is only the *consequence* of that sin that is lifted and carried away.

At this point, we are in a good place to describe forgiveness from a biblical perspective. Forgiveness is freeing someone from what they owe us for their actions. When you forgive someone, you no longer require any actions from them to make up for what they've done. Once a person is forgiven they no longer owe anything, not even an apology. If any action is required from the person they are not yet forgiven.

It must be noted, we can only forgive what is owed us. We cannot forgive on behalf of another person. Bryon cannot forgive our son, Jonathan, on Jen's behalf. Jen cannot forgive our daughter, Brenda, on behalf of Bryon. You cannot forgive another person on behalf of your spouse. You can only

---

[61] If you would like to read an in depth discussion of forgiveness, we recommend *Forgive & Forget* by Lewis B. Smedes.
[62] Theological Wordbook of the Old Testament, 1421.

forgive what has been done to you. That is what was so fascinating about Jesus. When he forgave, he forgave sins. All sins. He forgave what others had done to God because he is God. That was radical and upsetting to the religious establishment of the day (Mark 2:1-12).

For a marriage to remain healthy, forgiveness must come with restoration. The two concepts are related but distinct. Forgiveness means no longer holding a person's actions against them. Restoration means repairing what has been broken in the relationship because of their actions. Forgiveness means I'm not mad at you anymore. You don't owe me anything. I will not hold this against you. Restoration, on the other hand, means that I trust you with my whole heart again. I return all of myself to you. Our relationship is fully restored.

We feel it is important to note here that while forgiveness is a command on all Christians at all times, restoration is not. When you forgive a person, you do not necessarily forget what they have done. There are actions that can prevent restoration. Theft by a neighbor is an example of an action that must be forgiven but does not demand restoration. When a friend or colleague continually repeats a bad action, restoration may not be possible. A friend who perpetually gossips about you must be forgiven but that relationship may not be able to be restored. Restoration often cannot occur after abuse. When someone who should be trusted, such as a parent, teacher, or member of the clergy, hurts someone physically or sexually those acts should be forgiven, but those relationships quite often will never be restored. When crimes are committed, the police should be involved, but forgiveness must still occur. Forgiveness is separate from the legal consequences of behavior.

In marriage there are two things that we believe must be forgiven but may prevent restoration: infidelity and abuse. Through God's grace it may be possible to overcome either of these instances, but the break of trust in both of them is egregious. The relationship may never be restored. If the relationship cannot be restored, this does not necessarily mean the next step is divorce. There are options other than divorce. In a book like this, we cannot go into every situation. Our advice is to seek wise counsel from people that you trust that understand your faith, your situation, and the law in your state.

Biblical Ideal of Forgiveness

Forgiveness is clearly a biblical principle for our interactions with others based upon God's interaction with us. The Bible is full of examples of forgiveness. The story of Israel in the Old Testament is a story of repeated sin and forgiveness. The gospel is, of course, the ultimate story of forgiveness. The best instruction of how we should forgive is found in Matthew 18 and is given to us by Jesus himself.

Matthew 18 starts with Jesus' teaching on the process of addressing sin within the church. Yes, we know the church did not exist yet. The teaching is, however, clearly intended for the community that Jesus is forming during his earthly ministry that will continue after he ascends to the Father. The church is specifically referenced in verse 17. This is important because the teaching is about forgiveness and restoration among Christians.

Chapter 18 opens with a teaching about the great value God places on the members of his family and a process for restoration among believers. At the end of this teaching Peter asks Jesus a question, "Then Peter came to him and said, 'Lord, how many times must I forgive my brother who sins against me? As many as seven times?'" (Matthew 18:21). Peter likely thought he was being magnanimous. The Rabbis of the time likely taught that the number of times one was required to forgive another was three. Peter is offering to forgive more than double that requirement. In Hebraic culture, the number seven was also a symbol of completeness. In Peter's mind forgiving someone seven times would be complete forgiveness.[63]

Jesus saw the situation very differently from Peter. "Jesus said to him, 'Not seven times, I tell you, but seventy-seven times!'" (Matthew 18:22). The King James Version says 70 times 7. The actual number isn't Jesus' point, nor is it permission to stop forgiving another after 490 times. Jesus' point is that there is no limit to Christian forgiveness. This is the point of the Parable of the Unforgiving Servant that follows in verses 23-35.

If you're unfamiliar with the parable, take a moment now to read Matthew 18; we won't quote it completely here.

To summarize, a servant was forgiven an outrageous amount of money

---

[63] Michael J. Wilkins, *The NIV Application Commentary: Matthew*, (Grand Rapids, MI: Zondervan, 2004), 622.

by his master. The amount of money was so high there was no way the servant would ever be able to pay it back in his lifetime. The forgiven servant finds someone who owes him a significant amount of money, but not nearly as extreme as what he owed to the master. Commentators estimate that it would take a couple of months to pay off the debt. Once again, the actual numbers are not that important. What is important is what they represent. The first servant owed an amount he could never repay. He was owed by the other servant an amount that could be repaid in time. The first servant was impatient and refused to wait to be repaid and had his fellow servant thrown in a debtor's prison. Once the master discovers the unforgiveness of his servant he punishes that servant even more severely. Jesus ends the parable with a strong warning, "So also my heavenly Father will do to you, if each of you does not forgive your brother from your heart" (Matthew 18:35).

To fully understand and apply what Jesus is saying we need to look at the whole teaching, not just the segments. The first section (verses 1-14) discusses the equivalent value of every believer in God's eyes. No believer is greater than any other in God's eyes and he takes special care to bring those wandering away back to him. The second section (verses 15-20) addresses conflict between believers. As we have mentioned before, Christian marriage is a special relationship in the context of the church. In earlier chapters we talked about the equivalent value of husbands and wives. We have also discussed properly handling conflict in marriage.

Now we come to the conclusion of Jesus' teaching in Matthew 18. Peter thought that there was a limit to forgiveness. He thought that complete forgiveness was finite. Jesus said that Christian forgiveness is not finite because the cause and source of Christian forgiveness is the limitless, unfathomable, amazing forgiveness of God. Because God's forgiveness is without measure, Christians must forgive without limit and are also equipped by God to forgive without limit.

The point of the teaching here, however, is more than simple forgiveness that can lead us to avoid addressing the issues that hinder connection in the Christian community and oneness in marriage. In his commentary on this passage, David L. Turner says, "Disciples dare not allow this family to be disrupted by offenses, yet they cannot resolve offenses without a forgiving spirit."[64]

You dare not allow your marriage to be disrupted by offenses, yet you cannot resolve offenses without a forgiving spirit.

The Act of Forgiveness

Forgiveness is essential to human interaction. All humans suffer the effects of sin. All humans are selfish and will sin. All humans will, therefore, hurt someone. It is impossible to go through life without being hurt by another person. One day, when we are all living in God's kingdom on the new earth there will be no sin and no hurt. Until then, we must deal with the pain of being hurt. Until then, we must also wholeheartedly and continuously forgive.

Like love, forgiveness is an act, not a feeling. Forgiveness is an act of will. It is a choice. Let's look at the definition of forgiveness we provided earlier in this chapter. Forgiveness is freeing someone from what they owe us for their actions. Forgiveness is the choice to remove the debt you feel another person owes you.

As important as forgiveness is in Christianity in general and marriage in particular, we are amazed at how often we hear from people that they don't know how to forgive. While forgiveness is incredibly important, it is something that most churches presume you already know. There are a lot of sermons about how God forgave us in Christ. There are a lot of sermons about how important it is for us to forgive others. There are *not* a lot of sermons about how to forgive.

We think the reason that there are few instructional sermons on how to forgive is because most of those sermons would sound like an old Nike commercial, "Just Do It." Forgiving is actually very simple. It's not always easy, but it is simple. You forgive by choosing not to hold an action against someone. There's nothing magical about it. No special actions or formulas. Sometimes it helps to tell the person out loud "I forgive you." Saying the words, however, does not make it true. It is true when in your heart and

---

[64] David L. Turner, *Cornerstone Biblical Commentary; The Gospel of Mathew*, Vol 11, (Carol Stream, IL: Tyndale House Publishers, 2005), Kindle location 7658.

mind you acknowledge that the person does not owe you anything. You acknowledge in your heart and mind that what the person did was wrong but you no longer hold it against them. Then you act accordingly. You do not demand anything from them. You do not treat them as if they owe you anything. The damage may still be there. It may take a while for it to heal, but you do not require anything from them to heal the damage. They may want to help. They may want to "make it up to you." That is ok, but it is not something that you require or initiate. You allow them to respond out of their love for you, not to earn back your goodwill. Sometimes, their efforts will help you to forgive them; but whether they help you along with forgiveness or not, you must own forgiveness for yourself and then extend it to them.

Two things make forgiveness hard. First, it violates our sense of fairness. If forgiveness is in play, it is because we have been wronged. Our sense of fairness demands that things be set right. It's not fair that the wrongs done to us are not repaired or repaid. True! And that's the point. Forgiveness upsets the balance of fairness. That, of course, is the point. God forgiving us upset the balance already. When we forgive, we follow the example that God set for us.

Second, feelings of forgiveness do not always come right away. You may forgive someone. You may choose to remove the debt and not require any repayment but you may still feel like they owe you. That's ok. As we've discussed at length, we only have limited control of our feelings. There will be times when you forgive your partner and you don't feel like they are forgiven. In these cases you must choose to act in light of the truth of your choice, not the experience of your feelings. This is not "fake it till you make it." This is rather acknowledging both the truth of forgiveness and your human limits regarding your emotions. As you treat each other as forgiven, your emotions will follow. Over time, your emotions will catch up with the truth of your choices.

One final point: forgiveness may not be permanent. You may have to forgive the same thing multiple times before it sticks. In one moment you may have forgiven your spouse for that thoughtless comment or that disrespectful act. You may have decided that they do not owe you anything and are treating them accordingly. The next morning you may wake up and discover that your forgiveness has slipped. You may find yourself expecting recompense for what they've done. This is also ok. It just means you need to forgive them again. You keep making the choice to forgive until the choice has become permanent and you no longer need to re-forgive them for what they've done. Forgive then, day after day until the forgiveness sticks.

Forgiveness is Not Excuse

It is important to remember that forgiveness is not excusing, justifying, or allowing bad behavior. Forgiveness is not saying bad is not bad or hurtful acts are ok. To truly forgive, you must acknowledge that the thing done against you was bad.

God never says sin is not sin. God never says sin is ok. God acknowledges sin and chooses not to hold our sin against us. God acknowledges our debt and chooses not to make us pay it.

This means that sometimes you must have hard conversations about the hurtful things that have happened. You will need to address the words and actions that hurt you. Sometimes you might feel like it's the wrong thing to do but if your feelings are hurt; it must be addressed nevertheless. You will need to discuss how to prevent all those hurtful things from being repeated. Working through hurt and coming up with a plan to prevent it from happening again is not a lack of forgiveness. It is an act of love and restoration.

Conclusion

Forgiveness is fundamental to Christian life. Forgiveness is, therefore, fundamental to Christian marriage. From a Christian perspective, forgiveness is freeing someone from what they owe us for their actions against us. Forgiveness is not a feeling or emotion. Forgiveness does not require any special forms or phrases. Forgiveness rather is an active choice to not hold a bad act against somebody, choosing not to require them to make up for their action, and treating them accordingly. God's amazing extravagant forgiveness of us provides both the model and power of forgiveness. If you want a happy, healthy marriage that will last a lifetime, you must forgive your spouse. They will fail. They will hurt you. In the end, you have to choose how important your marriage is to you. If you want a thriving marriage, you must choose to forgive your spouse and your spouse must choose to forgive you.

Action step:

Discuss with your spouse:

- Is there anything that you need to forgive them for? Be open to anything they need to forgive you for.
- Is there anything that is festering that could be unhealthy in your marriage?
- How will you resolve anything that is between you so that your marriage may be restored?

POSTSCRIPT

For the past 20 chapters we have talked about Christian marriage. We have shared from our experience both in our marriage and from working with married couples in various contexts (legal, military, and ministry). We have seen a lot of good marriages. We have seen a lot of bad marriages. Because of our unique vocations, people have allowed us to look into their marriages and see the beauty and the mess. We have seen a lot and learned a lot about marriage. We hope the advice in this book gives you resources and encouragement to help you build a thriving marriage that will last a lifetime.

In this postscript we would like to make one final point. This is, perhaps, the most important point we make in the book. If you want to be a good Christian husband; if you want to be a good Christian wife; and if you want to have a good Christian marriage: *be good Christians.* At the end of the day it really is that simple. At the end of all his searching for meaning the author of Ecclesiastes said, "Having heard everything, I have reached this conclusion: Fear God and keep his commandments, because this is the whole duty of man" (Ecclesiastes 12:13).

Never be satisfied with your personal spiritual growth, or your spiritual growth as a couple. Continue seeking God and his righteousness (Matthew 6:33). Never grow weary of doing good (Galatians 6:9). Spur one another on to do the good works God prepared in advance for you to do (Hebrews 10:24, Ephesians 2:10). Then you will have a thriving marriage that will reflect Christ and also last a lifetime.

If you would like to contact us, you can email us directly at BryonJenHarvey@gmail.com.

grace and peace to you,
Bryon and Jen

Lightning Source UK Ltd.
Milton Keynes UK
UKHW041146231120
373920UK00011B/714/J